PUNJABI COOKING

Punjabi Cooking

PREMJIT T. GILL

STERLING PUBLISHERS PVT. LTD.

STERLING PUBLISHERS PRIVATE LIMITED
L-10, Green Park Extension, New Delhi-110016
G-2, Cunningham Apartments, Cunningham Road, Bangalore-560052

PUNJABI COOKING

© 1984, Premjit T. Gill

Reprint 1986

Reprint 1988

PRINTED IN INDIA

Published by S.K. Ghai, Managing Director, Sterling Publishers Pvt. Ltd.,
L-10, Green Park Extension, New Delhi-110016
Printed at Roopak Printers, New Delhi-110032

Preface

The improvement in taste of food has been an age-old passion with culinary experts. The changing world scene and values of life, when children are spending less time at home and learning even less from their parents, especially mothers, has created the need for cook books at home. But there are very few books giving details of the raw materials and the procedures of creating a good dish many people relish.

Punjabi food, as it is cooked from Delhi to Kashmir or Peshawar to Ganganagar and Kangra, by Punjabis around the world, has been explained, keeping in mind the international scene, by an experienced cook having scientific knowledge. The availability of the materials at hand in North America has been ·kept in mind. Flavouring and functional aspects of different foods, herbs and spices have also been detailed.

Of course, enjoyable food is the essence of good cooking, which is the outcome of experience and good planning. An elementary knowledge of different spices and basic ingredients is a necessary first step in that direction, which I have tried to provide in this book on Punjabi cooking. I owe my thanks to friends and relatives for helping me with their ideas. In this attempt, my husband Tarlochan and son Sundeep have played a big part in ınfluencing me to put my humble ideas in print. I aın highly obliged to Sardarni Swarn Kaur and Col. K.S. Sahi for their constant encouragement.

Contents

1 Presentation

Indian food varies from one region to the other just as languages, climate and customs do. Therefore, I will not claim to give you an insight into the art of Indian cooking. I shall only bring you some of my own favourites. Punjabi food or its way of cooking has not been represented fairly in Europe, North America or even outside Punjab in India or Pakistan. For this reason I intend to bring to my readers the good food of Punjab and the true spirit of Punjabis.

This book is intended not only for the western readers but also for the Indian readers who enjoy Punjabi food and wish to learn its method of cooking.

There is really no need to go looking for ingredients in special stores as I will mention some substitutes which are available in all supermarkets throughout the Punjabi world. Nor is there a need for any special utensils. A good cook usually always has heavy bottomed pots which are suitable for cooking.

Exact measures are seldom used in our cooking and a lot depends on the judgement, taste and experience of the cook. However, I have tried my best to work out every recipe in measures that are familiar to both the North American and the Punjabi. To suit your individual taste you can alter the recipes a little, eventually may be creating your own.

The Punjabi food preparation uses a number of methods of cooking—boiling, baking, sauting, steaming, frying, roasting, barbecuing and pressure cooking

Fats used could be either butter, margarine, cooking oils or ghee. *Ghee* is clarified butter and can be made simply by heating unsalted butter in a vessel on *medium heat* to evaporate the moisture When you can see through to the bottom, remove

it from the fire and strain. Cool and store in a covered bottle or
jar. This prevents it from getting rancid.

II

In India food is served in different ways It is presented
in accordance with the religious and traditional customs of the
various communities. In most restaurants and hotels food is
served on tables set with fine crockery and silver. In traditional
restaurants you may find yourself with food served on a banana
leaf or a leaf plate and with no cutlery at all In the religious
places you have to use your hands, only the right hand fingers
to break and eat the food Another style, most common in
Punjabi homes, is food served in a thali. One or more small
silver or steel bowls (katori) filled with different foods are
placed on a flat round matching tray. Rice, chutney and breads
are served on the tray alongside the small bowls. Indian food
does not need a lot of garnishing for decorative looks as the
food served in a thali itself makes it decorative enough with the
different colours and texture of varied items like rice, curry,
raita, sweet, bread, and dal. Every dish has a character and
taste of its own and therefore, I do not recommend that they be
served all in one plate, at the same time, but the latter, however, is more convenient in North America
You can use a lot of imagination when setting a table, as each
dish has a different colour and this does provide a lot of variety.
Alcohol does not blend very well with spiced food and I do
recommend plain water or lassi (buttermilk) as an accompaniment with food. Do not eat Indian food with a knife and fork.
The use of just a spoon is enough or when a spoon is not available
a piece of any bread can form a very suitable scoop (burki) for
eating curries and once you get used to eating a burki (scoop)
of phulka (bread) with curry you will enjoy it the most.

GLOSSARY OF SOME TERMS

Panir (ricotte cheese) is an important ingredient for
curries and sweets. For a vegetarian, the use of Panir has the
same protein value as the use of meat and is easily digestible
also. It can be obtained as follows. Boil 4 cups of milk and

squeeze half a lemon or add 2 teaspoonfuls of yoghurt or 1 teaspoonful of vinegar. Remove from the fire and strain through a cheesecloth. Drain out all water (whey) by hanging the cheesecloth tied to a water tap over the sink. The residue in the cloth is called panir. There is no exact English term equivalent for it. Ricotte or cottage cheese is the closest. Shape it into a square or round in the same cheesecloth and place under a weight (4-5 lbs) for a couple of hours so that it will be pressed into a compact slab. Remove the cloth and cut into squares or whichever shape required and use it either fried or as it is. The pieces should be cut about ¾″ square in size.

Khoa is thickened fresh milk and in North America I suggest a lot of recipes (Burfi plain or Besan) can be substituted with dried milk powder or if necessary can be obtained by boiling ½ cup of milk to which 4 cups of powdered milk is added. Blend in 2 tablespoonfuls of butter and remove from fire.

Dahi (Yoghurt) is an important ingredient in the preparation of curries and is also served with rice preparations by itself. Plain yoghurt sold in supermarkets is a good substitute. To prepare Dahi boil 4 cups of milk and cool till lukewarm. Beat thoroughly 2 tablespoons of yoghurt left out of the fridge overnight; mix into, the lukewarm milk, pour into a covered glass jar and place in a warm place overnight to set. A good place to leave it in is the oven after the day's work is over. When set, place in the fridge. Always put away a little yoghurt to start the next batch. It is practical to make yoghurt in several small containers and use one at a time, when needed. I usually make mine at home twice a week.

2 Herbs and Spices

It is my belief that the western mind will not easily understand the wisdom of our ancients in regard to the use of herbs and spices. India is the home of several fragrant herbs and spices but in every state all of them are not used. Some herbs and spices used in the South are never used in preparing food, when cooking in Punjab. As tastes differ in different regions of India, so does the use of herbs and spices and their combination; if, in North America or Europe, the people should have any difficulty selecting or combining different spices it must be understood that only experience will teach you what is the best that suits your taste. However, I will give you the recipe which is our favourite at home. Also I wish to mention some hints in connection with herbs and spices for their effective use by an average cook.

For Punjabi food you will regularly need to use coriander, cumin, cloves, cinnamon, cardamom, black pepper, red chilli powder or cayenne, turmeric and mustard. Also sometimes fenugreek, saffron and aniseed are used. Herbs are plants with soft succulent stems that whither away after flowering; plants that die down to the ground each year and do not have the remains of a woody or permanent stem above the ground. Herbs have aromatic properties and are sometimes used for medicinal purposes. In cooking, they could be used for garnishing or flavouring, for preparing herbal teas and beverages, herbal butters and vinegars, also used for perfumed soaps, making decorative sachets, incenses and candles and perfumes and for the purpose of dyeing. For drying, herbs should be cut just before flowering and dried in the shade, hung upside down in bunches, in an airy spot, or can be washed, drained, chopped fine and then dried on cheesecloth spread on a stool or flat surface in the shade.' Seeds are harvested when ripe.

A spice may be any strongly flavoured or aromatic substance, obtained from seed, root, bark, fruit or flower, that is used in much the same way as the herbs. Often the entire plant is called herb, while certain useful parts of the plant are called spice. For example the plant commonly called coriander, produces green leaves and stems that are used in cooking either fresh or dried and is called a herb. When the same plant goes to seed, the seeds are labelled as spice.

We tend to think of herbs as temperate climate plants that may be used either fresh or dried, while spices as being obtainable from the East and the tropics and are dried whole or cut and powdered. But nowadays even traditional spices such as ginger are grown in temperate climates or in home gardens.

Herbs and spices should be thought of as a complement to other substances and should be used in very small quantities. The real importance of herbs and spices to me is the flavour they impart to my cooking. They enhance the natural flavour of foods but one must use a lot of imagination, restraint and caution in their use. Experience alone will teach their discriminate use.

It is wrong to think that a real good curry is not obtainable in the West. We have lived here in Canada for 15 years and almost every night there is a curry dish on the supper menu. A good curry powder combination is essential to produce a good curry and is called garam masala. Many brands and names are available in the stores but I usually depend on my own recipe as the makers of these so called curry powders are all mixing different spices in different proportions. The ingredients for garam masala should be ground very fine and mixed well; it will store in an airtight container sometimes for years. Take out into a small bottle, the quantity to last you a couple of weeks at a time, so that the rest of it remains fresh in the airtight container.

Each province in India has developed a different cuisine which depends on what is grown and available within that area.

Turmeric (*Haldi*) should be used (not an ingredient of the garam masala) to give colour; must not be used with green leafy vegetables and beans. One must be careful not to spill turmeric, as its stains are difficult to remove. It is a tuberous perennial and is used in dry, powdered form. It is also used as an antiseptic for wounds in poultices and is considered a blood purifier.

A mortar and pestle or a grinding stone is very essential to grind small quantities of spices or herbs. Here, in North America, an electric grinder can be used for dry ingredients and a blender for others such as onion, garlic or ginger.

Ginger (*Adrak*) is really not a root; it is a perennial rhizome. It is used either fresh or dried and powdered. It is also used in crystallized form as candied or cooked with shortbread biscuits or *Nan khatai* (Butter cookies). Fresh ginger can be used either grated, blended in the blender or chopped very fine. It stores well in the freezer for a couple of weeks if kept in a plastic bag.

Saffron (*Kesar*) is used in sweets and rice dishes. It is very expensive and is the part of a flower grown in Kashmir. It is also used for skincare by young girls to clear the complexion; used also for dying clothes.

Garlic (*Lasan*) is a bulbous, perennial plant and is used as a flavouring herb. The thin skin or membrane of the bulb encloses up to 16-20 small pods called cloves which is not the same as the spice clove. It is grown by a method very similar to onions.

As with all other strongly flavoured herbs, garlic needs to be used with utmost discretion. For cooking, the juice can be obtained by pressing in a small garlic press. When only a small amount is desired the best method is to use either dried garlic powder or garlic salt or a few drops of juice extracted and kept in a bottle.

Garlic is taken for fever, whooping cough, flatulence, acne, pulmonary diseases, sciatica, asthma, tuberculosis, blood pressure, colds, diarrhoea, chest pain, and is also effective as a disinfectant and antiseptic when preparing poultices for open wounds. The oil in which garlic has been fried is a useful liniment to be used for rheumatic pains.

Alum (*Phatkari*) is used for preparing *Murabbas*—preserves from mango or cucumber. Also used in cooking white pumpkin (sweet *Petha*).

Asafoetida (*Hing*) is a gum obtained from a plant and should be used very cautiously as it has a very strong smell. It is used in preparing pickles, meat-balls and besan curry. Sometimes it is used fried in a little oil, when preparing *dals* (lentils).

Bay Leaf (*Tejpatta*) is a leaf of a species of laurel tree, used whole for flavouring soups, curries and pulaos.

Bitter gourd (*Karela*) is a vegetable to be cooked carefully because of its bitterness; when it is stuffed and shallow fried, it turns out into a delicacy Once you develop a taste for it you will always like it.

Coconut (*Naryal or Khopra*) is used fresh in the preparation of *burfi* (fudge) and in many other preparations. Also eaten as a fruit.

Basil (*Tulsi*) leaves have a strong flavour somewhat like cloves. It is a highly aromatic plant and is worshipped by the Hindus. Fresh or dried leaves are used in preparing tea. Dried leaves can be used as a garnish in meat and vegetable curries and also as air freshner and in making of incense.

Cumin (*Zeera*) is a seed used in seasoning yoghurt, vegetable and meat curries and is a constituent of curry powder. It is a symbol of fertility and has great medicinal value for strengthening the lining of the uterus.

Celery (*Ajwain*) Its green leafy part is used in salads, soups and tomato juice. It is also used in cooking fish, meat, vegetable curries and stews. Seeds have medicinal use in colic and stomach pain; in poultices for sprains and muscular aches.

Coriander (*Dhaniya*) greens are used in soups. stews and curries just like parsley. Powdered seed is a constituent of garam masala and is also used by itself in dals and soups. I have never tasted it myself with meat but have been told it makes a lot of difference when added to meat dishes. It has great medicinal value in constipation, nausea and flatulence. Coriander greens, green chillies with lemon juice and salt make a very good chutney.

Cloves (*Laung*) the most aromatic spice is the unopened flowerbud of the clove tree—available and used either whole or powdered to flavour soups, stews, curries or deserts. It is used in scenting soaps and perfumes and has medicinal value in relieving nausea and stimulates the appetite. Everyone for sure knows the effective use of clove oil for toothache. It is also used in flavouring tea.

Cardamom (*Elachi*) is very popular, used with double quantity of roasted fennel seeds to give good taste (chewing gum) and sweeten the breath after consumption of heavily spiced food or alcohol. It is one of the most precious spices in the world. Most countries have adopted cardamon in their own ways In India, however, it is used in perfumes, soaps, curries and sweets. Used in the preparation of special teas, it is a useful aid to digestion. The dried pods are the fruit of a plant. The skin of the pod is either very light yellow, green, white or black. Each pod contains about 16-18 tiny round black seeds, which can be used either powdered or whole Use in moderation as flavour is strong and a small quantity helps to keep flavour delicious.

Cinnamon (*Dalchini*) is the bark taken off from young branches of the cinnamon tree. It is used liberally in cookies, cakes, fruits and on butter toast. It is the most popular spice used in sweets and is one of the ingredients of garam masala.

Cayenne Pepper (*Degi Mirch*) is red pepper powder obtained from ripe dried capsicums. Sweet peppers are mainly used in addition to turmeric to give colour to vegetable meat curries and roasted meats.

Chillie Powder (*Lal Mirch*). The small green hot peppers grown in Punjab, Kashmir and the tropics are very pungent. One should be very careful in the use of chillie powder as it is twice as hot as cayenne. In India, chillies are used in the treatment of some diseases and is applied to open dog bite wounds and sometimes burnt in fire, with the superstition of it having the powers to chase away evil spirits. Over-used it can act as an irritant to the digestive system. I recommend its use only in pickles or in very small proportion in preparation of karelas or bitter gourd.

Dill (*Soa*). The leafy tops are used in soups, meat dishes and as garnishes in yoghurt dishes. In a 1/10 proportion, the leafy greens are a delicious addition in the preparation of *sarsoo* (mustard) da saag. The seed is used in pickling spices and also for flavouring soups and curries.

Fennel (*Saunf*). All parts of the plant are aromatic and are used for scenting soap and candles. The oil extracted is used for flavouring liquers. Roasted and in a combination with cardamom it is used as a breath freshner after heavily spiced food or alcohol is consumed. Used in sweet dishes also. The black variety of fennel is called aniseed and is used much the same way but more in savoury dishes, breads and cookies.

Fenugreek (*Methi*) is a yellowish hard seed and is used in preparation of pickles or garnishing *dals*, after frying in hot oil. Should be used in moderation because it is bitter if it is not fried well or not crushed and used in right proportion.

Nigella (*Kalonji*), onion seeds which are basically used only as a pickling spice and when making Nan (the king of Indian bread).

Mustard seeds (*Rai or Sarsoo*) are of two varieties—big and yellow and big, black and small. The yellow is used for seasoning or as a paste in relishes and preparation of poultices. The black is used for flavouring of dals and Kanji (a spicy carrot drink) and also for vegetable pickles. It is the dried seed of the mustard green and the oil is extensively used for preserving pickles and for body massage.

Mace (*Javitri*), flavour is the same as nutmeg and is used as a powder. Very useful for women after childbirth and therefore it is used in Panjiri. It helps the system to get regularized in menstrual problems.

Nutmeg (*Jaiphal*) is used as a flavouring in sweets and garnishing coffee. Should be used in powder form.

Poppy seeds (*Khuskhus*) The plant from which opium is obtained is not the same. It is used as a thickening agent in some curries. Milk made with soaked almonds, pumpkin seeds and poppy seeds helps to ward off the heat during the summer months; the drink is called Sardai.

Pomegranate seeds (*Anardana*) are dried seeds of the fruit pomegranate and are used to prepare chutneys and to flavour batters used for making pakoras.

Plum (*Alubokhara*) is the sun dried fruit used in curries and in preparing chutneys.

Olive oil (*Zetoon ka tel*) is not used for cooking in North India. The oil is used for massage of infants and the sick.

Mint (*Pudina*) is mainly used when fresh, for making chutney and garnishing yoghurt dishes and dips. The leaves, dried or fresh, are used in teas for nervous stomach upsets and colds. The dried leaves are used in garnishes also in vegetable and meat dishes especially with goat or lamb meat. Mint leaves give good flavour when cooked with new potatoes and peas. Dried leaves are good as decorations and in *pot pourri.*

Other important names not found outside of the Indian cooking.

Dried Mushrooms (*Guchian and Dhingri*). Rarely does the North Indian use fresh mushrooms. They are black or white mushrooms, sun dried after threading like a necklace and hung to dry in well ventilated areas. Cooked in a curry with either chickpeas or in rice pulaos.

Gram (*Chollae, Chickpeas or Garbanzo peas*): They have an almost indispensable place in the vegetarian cook's kitchen. There are 2 varieties; black and white. Usually the white is used in curries, salads, soups and roasted or fried all by itself as a hot snack with drinks. The black variety is roasted and eaten almost all over North India as the 'poor-mans' cereal. The husk of chickpeas removed, then ground into flour is called Besan or chickpea flour which has multiple uses in a Punjabi kitchen. Some of the uses being, as a binding agent in almost all the batters for frying pakoras, meat or fish. Very versatile in use, it makes a fudge called Besan. It is said people doing hard work with their brains, benefit by its use; it sharpens the memory.

Semolina (*Sooji*) **Cream of Wheat**: Used for sweet halwa and *pershad* in North Indian religious ceremonies. As a snack it is roasted lightly in butter or ghee and nuts and raisins are added with a little sugar called Panjiri. It keeps well for a long time in an airtight container; It is very useful, mixed with some spices and raisins for women after childbirth and also for convalescents.

Corn Flour (*Makki Da Atta*): No Punjabi family will feel comfortable until they have discovered where to obtain it as it is used in the preparation of *Makki di roti.*

Pulses (*Dals*) is cooked as a thick soup. It is indispensable in vegetarian kitchens because of the high protein content within. There are a lot of varieties — *Masoor, Moong, Urad, Channa.*

When you survey the spices available today, one is looking at products from all parts of the world and many of these for flavouring and their fragrance are taken for granted; they were once very costly treasures or not always available even at high prices. Throughout the centuries herbs and spices have been in great demand. Recently there has been a great escalation in the

popularity in the use of herbs and spices, but before, most
North Americans were unfamiliar with herbs and spices other
than parsley and a couple of others A lot of people now grow
or buy herbs for their healing and flavouring properties. There
has been intensive research and lots has been written ex-
ploring the subject of herbal medications and home remedies.
However, in this chapter I shall only mention how we can
experiment with them in the cooking of our fragrant spicy dishes
for which the West has sought the knowledge. Nothing that
I will mention here should be taken as diagnostic or pres-
criptive. Some persons could have allergic reactions to certain
herbs and spices, should this happen, consult a doctor. In
India herbs and spices have long been used as silent expressions
of one's sentiments and feelings. People valued some of them for
example, tobacco, tea, coffee and salt substitutes and also as
perfumes and flavouring. This does not take away their use in
various ways and methods of cooking.

There is a language that belongs to herbs and spices.

Herbs & Spices	*Significance*
Allspice	Compassion,
Aloe (Kuar-gandal)	Grief, affection,
Balm (Malham, Taskin)	Sympathy
Basil (Tulsi)	Good wishes
Bay leaf (Tejpatta)	Reward for merit, or
	I change but in death alone
Cloves (Laung)	Dignity
Coriander (Dhaniya)	Concealed merit
Cumin (Zeera)	Fertility
Dill (Soa)	Stability
Fennel (Saunf)	Worthy of praise
Mint (Pudina)	Virtue
Peppermint (Pudina desi)	Warmth of feeling
Nigella (Kalonji)	Love
Caraway (kala zeera)	Sincerity
Nutmeg (Jaiphal)	Unexpected meeting
Cardamom (Elachi)	Preference
Cinnamon (Dalchini)	Purity of love
Saffron (kesar)	Mirth, happiness
Celery (Ajwain)	Strength

Herbs & Spices	Significance
Mustard seeds (Rai)	Rage
Mace (Javitri)	Fertility
Fenugreek (Methi)	Overcome evil
Poppy seeds (Khus khus)	Inseparable
Pomegranate seeds (Anardana)	Esteem

Garam Masala

White cumin seeds	200 - 250 gm.
Black cumin seeds	100 gm.
Big cardamom seeds	
Cloves	50 gm. each
Cinnamon	
Bay leaf	a few

Pick and clean all the ingredients and grind them to a fine powder. Use, as required, in various recipes. Make a large quantity and stock in an airtight container. Use a small bottle to keep a week's supply for everyday use as some aroma of the garam masala diminishes every time the bottle is opened.

Curry Powder

To the above ingredients add coriander seeds—500 gm. and prepare the powder in the same way.

3 Breads

I take the liberty to mention a couple of breads I learnt to prepare from friends while in Canada and these have been accepted in the family.

Breads in India vary in different parts of the country according to the different grains and the resultant flours obtained from them. In Punjab, it is basically wheat and corn that is used. In North America wheat flour is graded into 3 different grades:

1. Fine, all purpose flour (Maida) used for cakes and pastries.
2. Wholewheat flour (Atta), used for bread; and
3. Cream of wheat (Suji) used as cereal.

The most popular of the breads used in Punjab is what we call phulka, roti or chapati, its size varies in each household. On special occasions, puries and parathas are prepared and served in much the same way as roti or phulka. Different kinds of flour can be used for making phulkas, parathas and puries. Wholewheat flour is mostly used in their preparation which makes them nutritious.

A Punjabi housewife takes pride in the way she kneads the dough. The most important step in preparing a good chapati, roti, puri or paratha is the preparation of the dough. If your dough sticks to your hands or the bowl after combining all the ingredients, keep on kneading with addition of more flour until it comes away clean from the bowl.

Chapati or phulka is the most popular of these unleavened breads to go along with most of the savoury dishes of Punjabi food. In North America it is gaining popularity as an edible wrapper for some spicy sauces or snacks. Sometimes a ball of dough can be slapped out between the palms of your hands to form the phulka. Special griddle (Tawa) is used to bake it, you could also use your frying pan instead of a flat griddle with success.

It is important to use wholewheat flour in breadmaking for an Indian meal. Sometimes you can try out wholewheat flour measure to measure mixed with all-purpose flour. The appearance will be a little more appealing to some of you.

The basic dough for chapati or phulka can be obtained by kneading in a large bowl, ¼ lb (225 grams) of wholewheat flour with cold water. Knead, gradually adding more water if needed, till the dough is pliable, soft and leaves the sides of the bowl. Sprinkle little water on the dough and leave it covered with a wet cloth for about 15-20 minutes or till you can get your curry ready. Knead again a little and you find the chapaties or rotis made out of this dough resulting better in appearance and taste. Divide the dough into 8-10 portions and roll each portion into a ball on the palm of your hand. Place on a flat floured surface and roll out swiftly into a thin and almost as round a circle as you can.

Put a tawa or griddle on the fire and when it warms up place this thin rolled out circle on it. About half a minute later turn it over to the other side. Brown spots will appear on the side which was on the tawa. This is as it should be. Turn it over again and apply pressure to puff it up. While one chapati is on the tawa roll out the next and repeat the process. Stack them on a plate and cover gently with a napkin. As each successive one gets cooked pile it onto the next, it keeps them warm also. Smear with butter on one side only.

Makki Di Roti (Cornflour phulka)

450 gm (1 lb) cornflour finely ground
2 tablespoons melted ghee
Some boiling water
Pinch of salt

Mix flour and salt. Caution is advised when mixing cornflour with the boiling water; use a large spoon for mixing Leave for about 10 minutes and then knead well into a soft pliable dough; roll out and prepare as for phulkas. Serve hot with ghee and sarsoo da saag (Mustard greens). Sarsoo da saag and Makki di roti is the famous special food of the Punjabis. A good drink to go with it is **Lassi** (diluted buttermilk).

Paratha (Shallow Fried Wheat Leavened Bread)

Prepare the basic dough as described above. Flatten and roll out a chapati. Smear the upper surface with soft ghee or butter, fold into half. Smear the new surface again with ghee or butter and fold again. Now the shape is like a triangle. Roll out to a thin cone or triangle shaped paratha and bake on the heated tawa, like chappati. When turned the second time smear a little ghee or butter and fry till crisp and golden brown. Parathas are richer than chapaties as they are shallow fried food. Should be served hot if you prefer to have them crisp. They can be eaten cold also but tend to lose their crispness when stored. Try giving them different shapes like square, round or triangle according to your wish but pay attention to the edges so that the smeared ghee in the centre does not ooze out.

Potato Paratha (Aluwala Paratha)

250 gm potatoes boiled with skins
Coriander green a few leaves
2 green chillies finely chopped
Small onion finely chopped
1½ teaspoon salt
½ teaspoon coriander seeds, (crushed coarsely)
½ teaspoon cumin seeds
1 teaspoon anardana (pomegranate seeds—crushed)
or 1 teaspoon amchur (dried green mango powder)
1 tablespoon ghee
½ teaspoon black pepper
½ teaspoon red pepper crushed

Boil, peel and mash the potatoes. Heat ghee and fry the onion to a golden brown; add the mashed potatoes and the rest of the ingredients after removing from fire It is enough for 6-8 parathas. Prepare the basic dough. Shape 2 small balls of dough, flatten and place in between one heaped tablespoon of the potato stuffing, press the sides together, round off, roll as for chapati and fry as described for plain parathas. Could be served hot or cold with yoghurt, lassi or with a cup of tea.

Stuffing for Cauliflower Paratha (Gobi)

Make as for Aluwala Paratha except substitute grated cauliflower (2 cups) for the mashed potatoes.

Stuffing for White Radish Paratha (Muli)

Take 2 cups of grated muli or radish squeeze out the water
and make mixture as for Aluwala Paratha. Caution has to be
maintained because it is not easy to manipulate and one needs
to have some practice with it; however, with a little care you
will be successful and will relish the taste.

Puri (deep fried bread)

It can be made with either the basic dough or mix equal
quantities of wholewheat flour and refined flour. To 2 cups of
this mix, add 2 tablespoons of melted ghee or butter and knead
to a soft dough but a little less soft than the basic dough. Puris
should be made quite small about 4"-5" in diameter and should
be rolled thin. Puris cook faster than chapaties and parathas
and are therefore, convenient to make when inviting more
people. Heat oil or ghee in a large pot or wok (karahi). When
hot, fry the rolled out puris in it one or two at a time. As they
bubble up to the surface of the oil, press down gently with a
(jharni) slotted spoon and they will puff up Do not overcook;
remove when slightly brown and drain on paper before serving.
It is best served hot. When travelling, it is an ideal food and
easy to carry. They are delicious even when eaten cold and do
not spoil for at least 24 hours.

Sometimes the dough for puris can also be obtained by
mixing equal quantities of wholewheat flour, refined flour and
cream of wheat. To each cup of the mixed flours, add one
tablespoon of melted ghee or butter Allow the dough to rest
for at least 2 hours before frying the puris.

Bhatura or Khamiri Puri (Deep Fried Bread)

1 packet or 1 teaspoon of yeast
1 cup milk;
1 teaspoon sugar
2 pinches of salt
$\frac{1}{2}$ lb (125 gm) refined, all purpose flour

Ghee or oil for frying
¼ lb (125 gm) wholewheat flour
A few grains of aniseed (Sauf) crushed coarsely

Prepare yeast with sugar and 2 tablespoons of warm water Mix together with the flour and salt. Prepare a dough with some warm milk. Knead the dough well to a soft consistency. Cover and leave in a warm place for about 2 hours or until the dough rises to about double its size. Knead the dough again with greased hands. In the meantime heat oil in a Karai or wok, and fry small puris in the same way, as plain puris, to a golden colour. Serve either hot or cold with meat or vegetable curry. Can also be eaten by itself. You could avoid aniseed if it is to be served only with curry When eaten as a snack, aniseed improves the flavour.

Urad Dal Puri (Peethiwali Puri)

½ cup urad dal
2 cups wholewheat flour
1 teaspoon cumin seeds
Salt to taste
1-2 green chillies
A pinch black pepper
½ teaspoon coriander seed
1 tablespoon oil or ghee
Oil or ghee for deep frying

Wash and soak the dal in water overnight Drain water and grind to a paste with as little water as possible Mix salt, pepper, coriander seeds, cumin seeds and chopped green chillies Fry this paste of dal (Peethi) in 1 tablespoon oil or ghee on slow fire, till the mixture is almost dry. Knead flour to a stiff dough with cold water. Make small balls and flatten in between the palms of your hand Put one tablespoon of peethi mix between 2 flattened rolls of dough and pinch together the edges forming into a ball again and then roll out like a small chapati on a floured surface keeping it a little thicker than chapati. Deep fry till golden brown like puris and serve hot with any chutney or plain yoghurt (Dahi).

Nan (Baked Leavened Bread)

½ lb (250 gm) refined flour (Maida)
1 teaspoon sugar
¼ teaspoon baking powder
2 tablespoons ghee
4 tablespoons yoghurt
1 egg
4 tablespoon milk
¼ teaspoon salt
1 packet or 1 teaspoon yeast
For sprinkling on the top: mix one tablespoon ghee,
1 teaspoon poppy seeds (Khuskhus) and 1 teaspoon onion
seeds (Kalonji). Can substitute 1 egg yolk for 1 tablespoon
of melted butter if desired.

Sift the flour and mix into it sugar, baking powder and salt.
Heat the milk and add to it yoghurt, yeast, ghee and egg. Pour
this milk mixture into the flour, a little at a time, until it is all
used up. Knead well for 1ᶜ-20 minutes or until smooth and
elastic. Add a little dry flour if the dough becomes too soft or
sticky. Cover and leave to rise in a warm place for about 2-3
hours or until the dough doubles in bulk. Knead well again and
divide into 8-10 parts. Flatten each ball between the palms of your
hand with the help of dry flour. When it is the size of a pancake
apply a little mixture of ghee, poppy seeds and onion seeds on
one side of the pancake and a little warm water on the other.
Stick the water moistened side on a hot griddle or tawa. When
one side is done, place the raw side or the poppy seed mixture
side up under a hot grill and brown evenly. Smear with ghee
and serve hot with either chickpea curry or meat curry. Nan
comes out better when baked in a traditional clay oven (tandoor)
than over a griddle. It could also be baked in a hot oven
(450° F) for 10 minutes or longer till it is cooked. Nan is best
served with kababs (dry meat balls).

Missi Roti (Mixed Bread)

1 cup wholewheat flour (atta)
½ cup chickpea flour (besan)
Salt to taste
1 teaspoon coriander (dhania) seeds, crushed coarsely

1 small onion chopped or
2 green onions chopped with some green chillies
A few coriander leaves chopped fine or
A few fenugreek (methi) leaves chopped fine
Butter to smear on the roti
Water to prepare dough

Mix the 2 flours, add salt, coriander seeds, chopped onion and greens and knead into a pliable, soft dough with water. Bake as for chapaties, only that it takes longer to cook. Serve with yoghurt or buttermilk for breakfast or brunch.

Papad

They are savoury, paper thin wafers eaten in all parts of India, although, the spices and size differ from province to province. In Punjab the papads are flavoured with peppercorn, whole and ground, in abundance. They are seldom made at home as the procedure is very tedious and laborious. It is more convenient to buy them from stores. Sometimes, an eldelry lady in the house, having plenty of time on her hands and sufficient energy and patience, makes them in a large quantity to last a year or two. The making of papads is a trade in itself. Usually they are sold in packets of a dozen or more with directions for cooking. There are three methods of cooking:

(1) Bake in moderate oven on the middle rack until crisp;

(2) Deep fry in hot oil. They need to be fried rapidly and care should be taken not to burn them. Lift out from the hot oil when done and place on a kitchen cloth or paper; with another cloth press down to flatten out and also to absorb all the extra oil.

(3) Rapidly and evenly roast on an open fire or barbecue. You could do it on top of a stove also. Place over a cake rack or something similar to keep the papad from touching the burners.

I would like to explain how papads are made. Urad dal is used for making them because it is very glutinous. The urad dal is ground fine and then blended with salt and cooking soda, mashed white pumpkin and cold water into a stiff dough. The dough is pounded in a mortar with a pestle. It is then kneaded,

mixing a little mustard oil at the same time. This dough is rolled
out into paper thin chapaties, cut to required size and shape
and dried spread out in the sun. A lot of ground chillies, pepper
and cumin seeds are added. After having dried they are
stored in airtight containers and used as an accompaniment to
any dish or by itself.

Occasionally they are made into fancy shapes. They are
also made with sooji or rice flour instead of urad dal. I do not
recommend you to try to make them at home but I would
certainly like you to taste some varieties available at an Indian
store. Ask for the mild variety.

4 Rice

All over India rice known as Chawal is revered and it commands a special place in a lot of religious ceremonies. Rice is also considered a symbol of fertility. Rice can be classified into long, medium and short grained varieties. In any Indian meal rice is the main attraction on the table. It can be boiled, steamed or fried. Basmati is the long grained rice and is the most popular even though it is more expensive than the other varieties. The medium and short grained varieties tend to stick together as they are moist and tender. The latter are more suitable for making sweet rice and flours. Rice used should be as old as possible. It can be served tastefully garnished either with yoghurt or curry. Sweet rice pulaos can be made to look colourful by adding raisins, pistachios and almonds. Saffron imparts a special flavour and a sweet yellow colour to it. Just before serving, the rice tray can be decorated with silver paper or *varak*.

Precautions to be taken while cooking

Never wash rice in hot water as it will destroy the food value and also break the grains. Wash in cold water. Start cooking at high heat and once it comes to a boil, complete the cooking on low fire till all the water is absorbed. To cook one cup of rice use 2 cups of water. Do not stir more than once while cooking and use a very heavy bottomed pot with tight-fitting lid on it.

The amount of water can vary with the quality of rice. One learns best by experimenting.

Pulaos and rice dishes are a good party fare as they can be prepared in advance. Just before serving cover the rice with lid or foil and place in a hot oven for 15 minutes.

Plain Boiled Rice (Ublae Chawal)

1 cup rice
2 cups water
1 teaspoon butter

Pick and wash the rice in cold water and soak for 15 minutes
in 2 cups of water. Boil on high heat and once it starts boiling
bring down to medium heat. Add butter and stir once. When
all the water is absorbed take off the heat and allow to stand
for 15 minutes before serving. Serve with yoghurt, meat curry
or vegetable curry.

Pea Pulao (Matar Pulao)

1 cup rice
½ cup peas
2 cups water
2 tablespoons ghee
1 onion and 1 tomato
2 cloves (laung)
1 cardamom (elachi)
½ teaspoon cumin seeds (Zeera)
½ teaspoon garam masala
1 or 2 bay leaves (tej patta)
Salt to taste.

Pick and wash the rice in cold water and soak in water for 15
minutes. Heat ghee and fry sliced onion till lightly brown. Add
peas, cardamoms, cloves, cumin seeds, bay leaves and garam
masala and cook for a few minutes. Drain the soaked rice and
add to spices. Gently stir in 2 cups of water and salt. Cook on
moderate heat till all the water is absorbed. Remove from the
fire and serve with sliced tomatoes, yoghurt or dal.

Savoury Plain Fried Rice—Basic I (Namkeen Chawal-I)

1 cup rice
2 cups water
1 tablespoon ghee
½ teaspoon salt or to taste.

Heat ghee and fry the washed rice for a few minutes or until grains become transparent, then opaque. Add 2 cups water and bring down the heat. Cook with tight fitting lid till water dries up. Remove from the heat and allow to stand for 15 minutes before serving.

Savoury Fried Rice—Basic II (Namkeen Chawal-II)

1 cup rice
2 cups water or any vegetable or meat stock
2 tablespoons ghee
½ teaspoon salt or to taste
4 cloves
½ teaspoon garam masala
½" stick cinnamon
2 cardamoms (elachi)
1 onion sliced fine
2 cloves garlic chopped fine

Heat ghee and fry the onion and garlic until golden brown. Add all the ingredients except water and cook for a few minutes. Then add rice and fry till grains become opaque (5-8 minutes). Add water or stock and cook with a tight fitting lid. When water dries up remove from the heat and allow to remain covered for 15 minutes before serving. These are the two basic recipes for rice and pulaos. Rice can be decorated with blanched almonds, slices of hard-boiled egg, tomatoes, coriander leaves (chopped fine) or fried onions. You could use peas (frozen or fresh). If using fresh, fry with the spices; if frozen, add with the water. In the same way cauliflower, capsicums and mushrooms or any other vegetable can be used. Cut mushrooms and cauliflowers into medium sized pieces and fry with the spices before adding rice.

Fried panir pieces can also be added to pulao before serving. I do not recommend the use of turmeric (haldi) in fried vegetable rice, however, there is no hard and fast rule.

Meat Biryani or Meat Pulao

For stock:
½ lb mutton or goat meat
1 teaspoon salt
2 bay leaves

1 large onion
4 cloves garlic
4 cloves
6 peppercorns (sabat kali mirch)
6 cups water

Clean and wash the meat, add salt, chopped garlic and onion, bay leaves, peppercorns, cloves and water. Cook in a pressure cooker for ½ hour. Allow pressure to drop and cook on medium heat till only 4 cups of water remains. Separate meat pieces from stock.

For pulao:
2 cups rice
4 cups stock
4 tablespoons ghee
1 large onion sliced
4 cloves
2 cardamoms
6 peppercorns
1 teaspoon cumin seeds
1″ stick cinnamon
1 teaspoon salt
1 teaspoon garam masala
10-15 almonds and cashewnuts
1 hard boiled egg
1 tomato
A few coriander leaves chopped fine for garnishing
2 green chillies chopped fine for garnishing

Brown the meat pieces in ghee and keep aside. Fry onion, garlic, cloves, cinnamon, cardamom, peppercorns, cumin seeds, garam masala and washed rice for 5 minutes or until grains become opaque. Add meat pieces, salt and the stock and cook over moderate heat until water dries up. Remove Biryani into a covered dish and leave in a hot oven for a few minutes. In India, it is customary to remove the pot from fire and leave on hot ashes. A few pieces of live charcoal are left on the lid of the pot to keep the rice hot, until required to serve. Garnish with chopped coriander, chillies, nuts, sliced egg and tomato or crisp fried onion. Serve with a yoghurt preparation or dal.

Chicken Pulao (Murgha Pulao)

6-8 chicken drumsticks (legs)
2 cups rice
4 cups water
1 large onion chopped or sliced
2 bay leaves
2 cardamoms
1″ stick cinnamon
1 teaspoon cumin seeds
1 teaspoon salt
1 cup mixed almonds and cashewnuts
Some coriander or parsley chopped fine for garnishing

Masala paste for marinating:

1 teaspoon garam masala
1 small onion
1 small piece of ginger
4 cloves garlic
1 cup yoghurt or ¾ cups buttermilk
4 cloves
2 cardamoms
½ teaspoon turmeric powder
8 peppercorns

Grind together the ingredients of the masala into a paste. Rub over the drumsticks and leave for 2 hours or even overnight. In Canada, I recommend making this marinate and keeping the chicken pieces in a canister or covered box in the fridge a night before using in the pulao. Fry sliced onion until golden brown and remove half for garnishing. Add all the spices and fry for a couple of minutes. Add the drumsticks, mix all together and gently cook for about 15-20 minutes. Add rice and then the water and salt. Stir well. Cover and cook over medium heat, until the water dries up. Remove from fire, garnish with nuts, onions, coriander and serve with a yoghurt preparation (raita) or dal.

It is a good idea to soak a few strands of saffron in warm water, pound in a mortar and mix just before the pulao is removed from fire.

Also turkey shrimp or duck can be substituted for chicken in the recipe.

Multicoloured Rice (Navratan Pulao)

Follow the Basic recipe II and double all the ingredients so as to have 2 cups of rice to cook instead of one.

Ingredients to be mixed into rice after it is cooked :

I cup boiled or frozen peas; fry in one teaspoon of butter. Add a pinch of salt, black pepper and a few drops of green colouring, squeeze ½ lemon then keep aside.

I cup firm red tomatoes and red pepper chopped fine. Add salt to taste: Add a few drops of red colouring then keep aside.

I cup panir cubes (ricotte cheese), fry to a golden brown, and keep aside.

Ingredients for Garnishing:

2 large onions, sliced and crisp fried to a golden brown colour
10-12 almonds blanched and fried lightly
10 cashewnuts
½ cup raisins
2 hard-boiled and chopped eggs (optional)
½ cup pistachio nuts (shelled)
2 or 3 green chillies (small hot) chopped fine
1 small piece ginger, thinly sliced and fried.

Cook 2 cups of rice as in Basic recipe II and divide into 3 parts. Colour one part by mixing the fried green coloured peas into it. Mix thoroughly and keep aside. Colour the second part of the rice red by adding the tomato and red pepper mixture. Mix thoroughly and keep aside. Leave the third part white and add the panir pieces to it, mix thoroughly and cook all these portions separately for few minutes on slow fire.

In the meantime, mix the ingredients for the garnish leaving out the hard-boiled eggs. Place this nut mixture in a large transparent pyrex or glass dish and spread over it layers of green, red and white rice one over the other. Sprinkle with chopped chillies and coriander leaves or parsley and garnish with chopped eggs. Serve with vegetable or meat curry or with a yoghurt preparation (raita)

Three Coloured Pulao

1 cup rice cooked as in Basic recipe II
½ teaspoon cumin seeds

2 fresh ripe tomatoes
½ cup coriander and mint leaves
4 green chillies
1 small piece ginger
2 cloves garlic
½ lemon (juice)
Salt to taste

Combine in a blender the mint and coriander with green chillies, garlic, ginger, salt and lemon juice. Keep aside.

Wash the blender and blend the 2 tomatoes with salt to taste and cumin seeds. Do not add water. Pour into a saucepan and cook until the liquid is reduced to half. Mix ½ teaspoon of paprika. The mixture should be thick enough to pour and mix with rice. Keep aside in a separate bowl.

Cook rice as in Basic recipe II and divide into 3 portions.

To one portion mix enough of the mint or coriander mixture to make it a deep green. To the second portion add enough of the tomato mixture to produce a pink colour. In a transparent pyrex or glass dish place the green rice at the bottom; then spread the red rice over it and lastly spread the white rice. Put the dish into a moderately hot oven until all moisture is absorbed. Serve hot with a yoghurt preparation or dal or vegetable or meat curry.

Sweet Rice (Mithe Chawal)

1 cup sugar
1 cup rice
2 cups water
2 tablespoons ghee
½ cup raisins
½ cup nuts. Either a combination of slivered almonds, cashews and pistachio nuts or just one of these, whichever is favoured
6 threads saffron
½ teaspoon nutmeg (jaiphal)
2 cloves
Seeds of 2 cardamoms (small elachi)

Prepare plain boiled rice using only 1½ cups water. Dissolve sugar in ½ cup water and add saffron to it to form a syrup. In another pan heat ghee and add rice to it. Pour the syrup all at once and stir gently so as not to break the grains of rice. Add raisins, nuts, cardamom seeds, crushed cloves and nutmeg. Turn heat on low and cook till moisture is absorbed. Remove from fire and serve either hot or cold, garnished with silver paper (vark).

Rice Pudding (Kheer)

8 cups milk
½ cup rice
1 cup sugar
¼ cup raisins
¼ cup chopped nuts
½ teaspoon cardamom powder
½ teaspoon nutmeg
2 tablespoons desiccated coconut (optional)
2 teaspoons rose water

Boil the milk. Clean and wash the rice. Pour the boiling milk on rice in another pot and allow to cook on low fire stirring occasionally. Be careful not to break the rice grains. When the rice is soft, add the raisins, sugar, chopped nuts and cardamom. Cook on slow fire until the pudding thickens slightly. Add rose water. Pour into a serving dish and sprinkle nutmeg, or coconut. Usually it is tasty when served cold, yet, there are some people who like it served hot with puris or Mal Purra (Pancake) on a rainy day.

Rice Flour Pudding (Phirni)

4 cups milk
½ cup sugar
4 tablespoons rice flour
1 tablespoon rose water
1 tablespoon raisins
½ teaspoon nutmeg
2 silver papers (vark)
10-12 blanched and shredded almonds and pistachio nuts
½ teaspoon cardamom powder

Boil the milk. Add the rice flour and cook gently on low fire.

Keep stirring, till the mixture thickens to a creamy consistency. Add sugar and cardamoms and cook till the mixture thickens again. Remove from fire and add rose water, halve the nuts and raisins and serve in glass bowls individually or in a large bowl. Decorate with the remaining shredded nuts and nutmeg. Can be served hot or cold as desired.

If rice flour is not available you can substitute rice paste made in the following way:

Take 2 tablespoons of rice, wash and soak in water for 2 hours. Drain water and grind very fine, in a mortar adding a few drops of water if required.

Rau Di Kheer (Rice Pudding with Molasses)

It is a seasonal pudding made when the sugarcane juice is extracted for making gur or jaggery.

½ cup rice
1 cup molasses (thickened, raw, condensed)
4 cups water
or 6 cups sugarcane juice (rau)
1 cup raisins (optional)
8-10 almonds or cashewnuts (optional)
½ teaspoon cardamoms, crushed
2 tablespoons desiccated coconut
1 tablespoon butter

Boil molasses with water or sugarcane juice (rau) and butter. Add washed rice and allow to cook over low heat stirring occasionally until rice is soft. Add raisins, cardamoms and nuts and cook gently, stirring constantly as it thickens. Remove from heat and add coconut and rose water. Serve hot or cold as desired.

Some like it hot, some like it cold and some like it in the pot at least one day old. (You can add ½ cup brown sugar and 4 cups water or ½ cup jaggery and 4 cups water).

Khichree

The chapter on rice will be incomplete if I did not touch on how to prepare Khichrees. Rice and lentils cooked for children and invalids is Khichree. It is easy to digest.

½ cup rice
½ cup moong or masoor dal
1 tablespoon ghee (refined butter)
1 teaspoon salt
5 cups water
½ teaspoon turmeric
½ teaspoon cummin seeds, crushed
1 small onion
2 cloves garlic, sliced

Pick, wash and soak the rice and dal together. Heat the ghee, fry onion, garlic and cumin seeds until onion is light brown. Drain the rice and dal and add to onions. Add turmeric and salt and fry till the rice is opaque. Add water and cook on moderate heat until the rice and dal is soft and consistency is like a thick porridge. Serve with yoghurt or just by itself.

Plain Khichree

½ cup rice
½ cup masoor dal or moong dal
½ teaspoon turmeric
½ teaspoon cumin seeds powdered
6 cups water and
½ teaspoon salt.

Pick and wash the rice and dal. Add water, salt, turmeric and cumin seeds. Cook over low heat until consistency of porridge is reached.

Plain khichree is served hot to convalescents and small children changing over to solids. When not serving to the sick you could add 1 tablespoon of butter. Cold khichree is eaten with yoghurt (dahi) or (lassi) buttermilk. Bajra can be substituted for a dal.

5 Salads and Yoghurt Dishes

SALAD AND RAITA

No Punjabi meal is complete without a yoghurt dish. Raita is a combination of vegetables and/or fruits with plain yoghurt and seasoning. Easily prepared, they stimulate the appetite and aid in digestion. Raitas are also delightfully tasty. They can be part of a meal or can be had as a snack in between meals.

Onion and Tomato Salad (Kachumber)

2 green chillies (optional)
1 large onion
2 ripe firm tomatoes
1 teaspoon vinegar or ½ lemon, juice extracted
Salt to taste
Coriander leaves, a few

Sprinkle salt on the sliced onion and keep aside for a few minutes. Chop tomatoes into bite size. Wash the onion under cold water and mix with tomatoes, chopped chillies, chopped coriander and vinegar or lemon juice. Chill and serve with food as a salad.

Onion, Tomato and Cucumber Salad

2 medium onions, sliced
2 medium tomatoes, sliced
1 cucumber, peeled and sliced
2 green chillies, chopped or slit
1 hardboiled egg, sliced (optional)
Pinch of salt and pinch of black pepper

Either toss all ingredients and chill before serving or arrange in layers. Sprinkle salt and serve.

Potato Salad (Alu)

2 medium boiled potatoes
2 green chillies, chopped fine
Some coriander or mint leaves, chopped fine
Salt to taste
½ teaspoon roasted and powdered cumin seeds
A pinch of black and a pinch of red pepper
½ cup yoghurt or sour cream
½ cup chopped spinach.
Mixture of ½ cup chopped cashewnuts, sunflower seeds and
chopped almonds.

Chop boiled potatoes and mix with chopped coriander
leaves or mint leaves and spinach Add salt, cumin and pepper powder. Mix with whipped yoghurt or sour cream and
sprinkle nuts and sunflower seeds. Serve with mint chutney or
tamarind chutney.

Cabbage Salad (Patta gobhi)

½ head cabbage, shredded fine (Red)
1 tablespoon oil
1 lime or ½ lemon, juice extracted
1 capsicum or 2 green hot peppers chopped fine
½ teaspoon cumin seeds roasted and ground
½ teaspoon mustard seeds (black)

Heat the oil and put mustard seeds in it Add the shredded
cabbage (preferably red) salt, pepper and cumin powder, stir-fry
briskly for a couple of minutes Remove from the heat and add
lemon juice. Serve either cold or hot with pakoras or samosas.

To the above recipe, add ½ cup of plain yoghurt and mix
well. Refrigerate a few hours before serving with crisp fried
foods. To make it more colourful, add red or green sweet pepper
chopped very fine before removing from the heat. Few raisins
can also be added.

Coleslaw (Patta gobhi, gajar)

Slaw:
1 small cabbage shredded or chopped
1 onion

1 carrot
1 green pepper } Sliced or chopped fine
1 or 2 stalks of celery, chopped or shredded fine.

Sauce:
½ cup water
½ cup vinegar
½ teaspoon celery seeds
½ teaspoon mustard seeds crushed
½ cup sugar
½ teacup khuskhus
¼ teaspoon garam masala
Salt and pepper to taste

Garnish:
1 tablespoon raisins
½ cup sour cream or yoghurt

Mix together and boil all the ingredients for the sauce. Drain and keep aside to cool.

Mix all the ingredients for salad — coleslaw. Pour sauce over coleslaw and allow to infuse for at least 2 days in an airtight container (glass preferred). Leave the container in the fridge. When ready drain out the excess sauce and mix in ½ cup of plain yoghurt or sour cream and garnish with raisins. Serve as a salad with crisp fried foods.

Salad Dressing

2 lemons, juice extracted
1 teaspoon salt
1 tablespoon honey
½ teaspoon chillie powder
½ teaspoon celery seeds powdered
4 mint leaves, chopped fine

Mix all the ingredients thoroughly and store in a jar until ready to use. The dressing can be used for any tossed salad.

Bean Sprouts (Pungari Dal)

Moong dal, urad dal and chickpeas can all be used for sprouting. Each can be used by itself or in a combination.

To sprout beans take 1 cup dal. Clean, wash and soak in

water. Cover and leave aside for about 24 hours. Drain all the
water and place the dal in a cheesecloth or a square muslin piece.
Tie loosely and keep aside in a warm dry place. It could be kept
in an empty coffee jar (coloured) or in the corner of a cupboard
or in the oven if not to be used. If they are covered, warm and
in the dark they will sprout in about 24 hours. When ready to
use, sprinkle a handful on tossed salad or chopped spinach and
mushrooms. When sprouting any dal put in a few fenugreek
seeds (methi) also in it to sprout at the same time; this gives
a good flavour to the sprout mixture.

Bean Sprout Salad (Pungari Dal da Salad)

2 cups bean sprouts
½ cup raisins
1 tablespoon mustard oil
½ teaspoon cumin seeds
Pepper and salt to taste
½ lemon, juice extracted
1 small onion chopped

Heat the oil and fry cumin seeds, till brown. Add the sprouts,
chopped onion, salt and pepper to taste and toss briskly for
about 5 minutes. Add raisins. Remove from the fire and add
lemon juice. Serve by itself or with a meal.

Potato with Yoghurt (Alu Raita)

1 small onion chopped fine (optional)
1 large boiled potato
2 cups yoghurt
½ teaspoon salt
1 pinch black pepper
½ teaspoon cumin seeds
1 green chillie and a few coriander leaves

Beat the yoghurt, salt, pepper and cumin seeds together to a
smooth consistency Peel and chop the boiled potato into small
cubes. Add the potato and onion to the yoghurt and garnish with
green chillies and coriander chopped fine. Serve with parathas,
rice or curry Can also be used as a dip for vegetable salad or
chips and pakoras.

To create variety, tomato, capsicum or carrot (shredded) can also be added along with potatoes. Make sure you add more salt for extra vegetables added.

Cucumber with Yoghurt (Khira Raita)

1 medium cucumber
2 green chillies
Salt and black pepper to taste
Few leaves of coriander
$\frac{1}{2}$ teaspoon cumin seeds, powdered
2 cups yoghurt

Peel and grate the cucumber. Beat the yoghurt, cumin (zeera), salt and pepper thoroughly until smooth and creamy. Add the grated cucumber and chillies and garnish with chopped coriander. Serve chilled with stuffed parathas, rice or as a dip with fried foods.

Marrow with Yoghurt (Ghia da Raita)

$\frac{1}{2}$ cup water
$\frac{1}{2}$ lb (225 gm.) vegetable marrow
2 cups yoghurt
$\frac{1}{2}$ teaspoon cumin seeds, ground
A few leaves of coriander, mint or parsley
Salt and pepper to taste
1 green hot pepper (optional)

Scrape and grate the marrow. Boil in $\frac{1}{2}$ cup water until tender and water evaporates. Keep aside to cool Beat together yoghurt cumin, pepper and salt to a smooth consistency. Add marrow to yoghurt, mix and garnish with chopped coriander or mint or parsley and serve chilled with a meal or rice or parathas, or as a dip with fried foods.

Pakories

2 green chillies chopped fine
$\frac{1}{2}$ cup chickpea flour
2 cups yoghurt
Salt and pepper to taste
$\frac{1}{2}$ teaspoon cumin seeds

Water to make batter
Ghee for frying

Mix chickpea flourand one tablespoon ghee with water to
make a batter (ghol) of dropping consistency (not too runny).
Heat ghee and deep fry the batter dropped through a slotted
spoon. Remove pakories or boondies from the ghee and soak in
hot water for a couple of minutes Remove from water and
squeeze gently, keep aside to cool This enables the excess ghee
to be removed. Beat yoghurt, salt, pepper, cumin seeds and
chopped green chillies thoroughly and add the cooled pakories.
Mix well and serve chilled with crisp fried foods, parathas or
rice. Also served as a dip or by itself along with mint and
tamarind chutney.

Dal Patties in Yoghurt (Dahi Baray)

1″ ginger chopped fine
2 cups yoghurt
½ cup urad dal with skin
2-3 green chillies
Some chopped coriander
1 large onion chopped
½ teaspoon garam masala
½ teaspoon chillie powder
Salt and pepper to taste
Ghee to fry

Clean, wash and soak the dal overnight. Wash several times
to remove the husk Blend in a blender or grind on a grinding
stone until a coarse thick batter is obtained Be careful to use
only enough water to blend, otherwise the mixture will be
too runny and not suitable to make the bara. Mix ginger,
onion, garam masala, chillie powder with salt and pepper to
taste. Keep aside for an hour. Beat thoroughly until batter becomes light and fluffy Make into a round cutlet shape with
moist hands. Usually the shape is like a doughnut. Deep fry
carefully to golden brown. Remove from oil and soak for
5 minutes in warm water to remove excess fat. Squeeze gently
and keep in a serving dish to cool. When cold pour over
beaten yoghurt in which salt has been added. Garnish with

green chillies and coriander leaves. Serve with tamarind chutney either with a meal, or as an appetizer or by itself as a snack.

From this recipe you could omit the yoghurt and serve baras without soaking in water as a snack with tea or coffee.

Eggplant Raita (Baingan da Raita)

1 large eggplant about 1 lb
1 onion chopped fine
2 green chillies chopped fine
Pepper and ½ teaspoon salt to taste
Some coriander leaves chopped fine
½ teaspoon chillie powder
½″ (1.25 cm) piece ginger chopped fine
2-3 cloves garlic chopped fine
1 tablespoon ghee
2 cups yoghurt
1 small tomato chopped fine
½ teaspoon garam masala

Prick and bake or roast or boil the eggplant in a hot oven at 450°F, until skin is charred and the eggplant is tender. Remove the skin and mash the eggplant. Heat ghee and fry onion until light brown. Add the garam masala and ginger and fry a few more minutes. Add the eggplant mix and all other ingredients except yoghurt and tomatoes. Cook rapidly stirring all the time for about 10 minutes. Remove from the fire and keep aside to cool. Beat yoghurt and mix with finely chopped tomatoes. Add eggplant mixture and mix thoroughly Serve cold with a meal or with parathas, puris, rice or by itself; also as a dip. It could be garnished with chopped mint or coriander. The same recipe can be used for grated zucchini substituting it for baked eggplant.

6 Vegetarian

VEGETABLES

In India vegetarianism is second nature to a lot of people. Even though the Punjab is basically a meat-eating province, one finds many vegetarians there too No party is complete unless it caters specially for the vegetarians. Vegetables are grown in abundance in the Punjab and, therefore, it provides the initiative to experiment and include in the diet all the good fresh vegetables.

The vegetables can be cooked either in a curry or as a bhujia (dry vegetables). It is not advisable to camouflage the real taste with heavy sauces. Emphasis should be laid on simple preparations so as to keep intact all the nutrients.

Vegetables, whenever possible, should be obtained fresh. The eggplant (brinjal, baingan) is a great favourite in Punjab and is cooked in different ways. Another very popular dish is the 'Saag', leafy green vegetables cooked and blended well with corn meal. There are different kinds grown in Punjab and can be cooked with potatoes, onions, or by themselves.

Vegetables must be fresh and clean. Cooking time of vegetables varies and depends a lot on the size, freshness and the season. Vegetables should never be overcooked, as long cooking destroys crispness, freshness, colour and nutritive value. Do not soak vegetables in water for a long time. When boiling use as little water as possible. If you have extra water save it for use as stock for vegetable curries, soups or dals. Immerse vegetables in boiling water when required to cook and cook only until tender. Green vegetables will keep their colour if cooked without a cover until half done Stir only when necessary as too much stirring breaks the protective skin and they tend to loose their vitamins.

Vegetable Curry Masala (Wet)

Cooking a vegetable curry is quite a job in itself Although, it is a common practice to follow the rule of each recipe separately yet one can make a masala paste and keep in the fridge for use in small quantities at a time. I often prepare mine, a few days before, if I know I will be expecting guests or if I am too busy with other things that do not allow me enough time in the kitchen on weekdays.

2 lb (900 gm) onions chopped
1 lb (450 gm) garlic chopped
¼ lb (110 gm) ginger chopped or grated and kept separately
5 tablespoons ghee or oil
1 tin canned tomatoes or
4-5 large ripe tomatoes
1 tablespoon cumin seeds
2 tablespoons turmeric

Grind the onion and garlic to a smooth paste If using a blender add as little water as possible. It is preferable to either grind them in a mortar and pestle or grate onions andc rush garlic. Heat oil or ghee and add cumin till it pops, then add the onion paste and fry until golden brown. Add the turmeric and stir thoroughly. Add the tomatoes and ginger and cook until a smooth thick paste is obtained. Cool and store in a canister with a tight fitting lid. Use as required for all vegetable curries.

Potato, Pea and Panir Curry (Aloo Matar Panir)

1 large potato cut into 8 pieces
1 cup fresh peas
12-14 pieces of panir (refer to chapter 1)
½ cup yoghurt (dahi)
¼ cup wet vegetable curry masala
2 tablespoons ghee or oil
Some chopped fresh coriander leaves
1 teaspoon salt
1 teaspoon chillie powder
1 teaspoon garam masala
4 cups water

Heat the ghee and fry panir pieces to a rich golden colour.
Keep aside Add ½ cup vegetable curry masala and stir for
a couple of minutes on slow fire. Add the fresh peas and cut
potatoes and quickly stir for about 5 minutes, taking care not
to allow masala to catch at the bottom of pan. Add the salt,
chillie powder and panir pieces and water and allow to
simmer until water is reduced to half or until vegetables are
tender. Add the well beaten yoghurt and cook for another 2
minutes. Sprinkle coriander leaves and garam masala, mix well
and remove from the fire.

Serve as a main dish for vegetarian meals along with phulka,
puri, parathas or plain rice The panir pieces get swollen and
look like tender meat chunks floating in the curry.

The same procedure could be applied to make potato and
panir curry or potato, chickpeas and panir curry. Instead of
panir you could use mushrooms cut into halves or hardboiled
eggs. If using hardboiled eggs add whole hardboiled eggs just
before the yoghurt. Before serving food, cut eggs into half and
arrange decoratively.

Punjabi Mustard Green (Sarsoo da Saag)

1 lb (450 gm) mustard greens
1 lb (450 gm) spinach
One handful dill greens (soa)
2 onions chopped fine
1" (2.5 cms) piece of ginger grated or chopped fine
4-6 cloves garlic chopped fine
4 tablespoons ghee or butter
4-6 green chillies chopped fine (optional)
½ cup cornflour
3 cups water

Clean, wash and chop mustard greens, spinach and dill.
Boil water, add salt, chopped greens and cook over slow fire
until tender and enough water remains to keep greens together.
If the greens are not tender and water dries up, add a little
more boiling water to cook completely. Ordinarily it takes
around 2 hours but in a pressure cooker it takes 15-20 minutes.
Make a paste of cornflour with a little water and blend together
with the cooked greens away from the heat. When blended

thoroughly return to heat and cook 5 minutes more, being careful as now it could bubble out and splash; if you do not cook now for 5 minutes more the cornflour will not be cooked and will taste gritty while eating Cover and remove from fire, keep aside until tarka is ready. The tarka process is explained here in detail.

Tarka: On low fire heat the ghee, add onion, garlic and ginger and fry until golden brown. Add chopped chillies and pour over the blended greens. Return to the fire, stir vigorously for a couple of minutes and remove. Serve with Makki di (Corn) Roti and lassi (buttermilk). When cooked, saag should have the consistency of a thick porridge. Cook spinach and broccoli in the same way.

Eggplant Bharatha (Brinjal, Baingan)

1 large eggplant (1½ lbs or 775 gm)
2 large tomatoes chopped
2 large onions chopped
4 cloves garlic chopped
1" (2.5 cms) piece ginger grated
1 teaspoon salt
2 tablespoons ghee or oil
1 tablespoon garam masala

Wash, prick and roast the eggplant on a barbecue or boil on the stove until tender. Peel and mash. Heat the ghee and fry onions, garlic and ginger until golden brown, add mashed eggplant, salt, chillie powder and tomatoes and stir-fry until all moisture is rapidly absorbed and 'Bharatha' leaves the sides of the pan. Add garam masala and remove from the fire. Serve garnished with chopped coriander or mint leaves and green chillies For variety and colour, you could add a handful of frozen or boiled peas along with mashed eggplant. Serve as an appetiser or as an accompaniment to a meal with phulka.

Potato Bhartha

1 lb (450 gm) potatoes (new preferred)
1 large onion chopped fine
1 teaspoon salt
2 tablespoons ghee or butter

1 teaspoon garam masala
½ teaspoon cumin seeds
Chopped green chillies and coriander leaves to taste

Wash, boil, peel and mash the potatoes. Heat the ghee,
fry cumin and then add onion and fry until light coloured.
Add mashed potatoes, salt and garam masala. Cook for 5-7
minutes. Add chopped chillies and coriander. Serve as an
accompaniment to a meal or on a hot buttered phulka or a toast
as a snack. Add a few frozen peas to make it more colourful.

Peas and Ricotte Cheese (Matar Panir)

1 cup peas (boiled or frozen)
1 cup ricotte or cottage cheese (panir) crumbled
1 tablespoon ghee or butter
1 teaspoon garam masala
1 teaspoon cumin seeds
¼ teaspoon chillie powder
Dash of turmeric
2 chopped green chillies and some chopped coriander

Heat the ghee, add cumin till it pops. Add the turmeric, peas,
garam masala, chillie powder and fry for 5 minutes. Add crumbled panir and stir-fry for a few minutes. Add coriander and
green chillies. Remove from the fire and serve with a meal or use
in samosas and patties instead of mincemeat. When using for
patties or samosas do not stir-fry too long as further cooking
will be done inside them.

Stuffed Capsicums (Bhari Simla Mirch)

4 washed and seeded capsicums of equal size.

Capsicums can be stuffed with either mincemeat or, mincemeat and peas, or potatoes, peas and carrots or peas and
panir or whatever else you can think of as a good combination. Place tightly stuffed capsicums in a pan. Baste with a
little butter or ghee and bake for 30-45 minutes or until firm yet
tender. Serve garnished with chopped coriander, sliced tomato,
sliced hardboiled egg or fried potato fingers.

Stuffed Tomatoes (Bharven Tamatar)

4-6 same sized tomatoes
1 tablespoon butter or a batter of ½ cup besan (chickpea flour)
Salt to taste
1 tablespoon coriander seeds coarsely crushed
Ghee or oil for frying
Water to make batter

Wash and cut a narrow slice off the top of each tomato. Loosen the pulp. Place them upside down to drain. Use this pulp in any vegetable or soup. Stuff tomatoes like capsicums with either mincemeat, curried mincemeat and peas, potatoes or whichever filling is desired. Place the top slice on tomato and keep aside.

Batter:

Mix the besan, salt and coriander seeds with a little water and make a thick batter. Dip the stuffed tomatoes in batter being careful not to lose the lid of tomatoes and fry on high heat in a heavy bottomed frying pan. Remove when light brown and serve garnished with coriander leaves or with a tossed salad. A very good accompaniment to any meal. It can also be baked in a hot oven without dipping in the batter.

Stuffed Potatoes

Another vegetable suitable for stuffing is potatoes (can be held together with a toothpick). Half boil potatoes and remove the skin. Cut lengthwise in the middle. Scoop out to make a hollow. Stuff with any curried vegetable, join the two pieces with 2 toothpicks inserted on either end. Arrange in a dish and bake for ¼ hour or fry carefully and serve garnished with mint, parsley or coriander. The stuffed potatoes can also be simmered in some vegetable curry masala and served with plain rice. Alternately, arrange in a dish and bake for ½ hour along with the vegetable curry masala. It is a very delicious dish.

Stuffed Squash (Bharvan Kaddu)

All varieties of summer squash can be prepared by this method. Peel squash and cut in two horizontally. Scoop out the

seeds and pulp. Stuff enough of any filling and sprinkle liberally
with breadcrumbs, butter and tomato pulp mixed together. Bake
in an oven at 350° F for ½ hour or more till done. Then broil
for the next 10 minutes. Sprinkle a little grated cheese just a
few minutes before removing from the oven.

Stuffed Eggplant (Bharvan Baingan)

Select large, even-sized eggplants. Boil for a few minutes in
salt water to make them a little soft Cut lengthwise into two
and scoop out the pulp to make hollows. Use scooped out
pulp to mix with any bhurji you desire (potato, peas and carrots
is a good combination). Sprinkle the top with a mixture of breadcrumbs, tomato pulp and butter. Bake at 350°F for ½ hour and
then broil for next few minutes till a little brown. Add grated
cheese just before removing. Allow the cheese to melt. Remove
and serve garnished with onion slices or onion rings.

Stuffed Bitter Gourd (Bharvan Karela)

1 onion+4 cloves garlic ground to a paste
6 small karelas, even sized
4-5 tablespoons ghee or mustard oil
1 tablespoon amchur (dried mango powder)
½ teaspoon coriander seeds ground
1 teaspoon cumin seeds ground
1 teaspoon garam masala
Salt to taste and thread to tie the karelas
Instead of amchur pomegranate seeds can also be used,
  soaked overnight and ground with the onion paste.

Scrape the karelas until the surface is smooth. Make a slit
and remove any hard seeds Rub salt inside and out, being careful not to break the karelas into two. Keep aside for few hours
or better still, overnight. Wash the karelas gently in water and
squeeze dry. Heat 1 teaspoon ghee and lightly brown the onion
paste Mix in all the other masalas and keep aside to cool. Stuff
into karelas and wind some thread around to keep the masalas
in. Heat oil and stir-fry until lightly browned all over. Remove
and unwind the thread gently and serve with dals, yoghurt
dishes and phulkas or parathas. Karelas have a slightly bitter
taste and one cannot expect children to like them right away.

Stuffed Okra (Bhindi Masalewali)

1 lb okra, (Lady's finger or bhindi)
2 tablespoons dried mango powder (amchur)
1 teaspoon chillie powder
1 teaspoon cumin seeds powdered
1 teaspoon coriander seeds powdered
1 teaspoon garam masala
3-4 tablespoons oil
Salt to taste

Wash, dry and cut off the heads of okra. Make a slit length-wise into each and stuff with the dry ingredients mixed together. Heat oil and gently put the stuffed okra. Use a wok or karahi and briskly fry the vegetable for a few minutes. Cover and cook on low fire, stirring occasionally. Serve with dal, yoghurt dishes, phulka, paratha or rice garnished with chopped coriander leaves.

Okra and Onion (Bhindi Pyaz)

1 lb (450 gm) okra
2 medium onions (cut lengthwise thickly)
4 tablespoons oil
1 teaspoon garam masala
1 teaspoon cumin seeds ground
1 teaspoon turmeric
½ teaspoon chillie powder or 3 green chillies chopped

Wash and dry the okra. Cut into ½" (1.25 cm) pieces discarding the heads and stringy stems. Heat oil, add turmeric, cumin, salt, garam masala and chillie powder. Carefully add sliced onion and fry for a few minutes, then add okra pieces and briskly stir-fry for a few minutes. Cover and cook another 5 minutes and remove from the fire when cooked. Leave aside, without taking off lid for 10 minutes and be careful when you remove the lid, so that the steam formed on the inside of the lid does not fall into the pot. Garnish with chopped coriander and serve with phulka or parathas.

Bitter Gourd and Onion (Karela Pyaz)

4 medium karelas
2 onions medium sliced thickly

1 teaspoon amchur
1 teaspoon turmeric
1 teaspoon chillie powder
1 teaspoon garam masala
Oil for deep frying
Salt to taste
2 chopped green chillies

Scrape the karelas to a smooth finish, and slice thinly. Apply abundant salt and keep aside for a few hours or overnight. Wash well in cold water and squeeze out moisture. Heat the oil and fry karela pieces to a light colour. Heat 1 tablespoon oil in a pot and fry onion, turmeric, garam masala for a few minutes and add fried karelas to it and cover Cook for a few minutes on low fire stirring occasionally until tender. Add amchur and chopped chillies or chillie powder. Serve with yoghurt dishes or dals with tandoori roti or parathas.

Mixed Vegetables (Milijuli Sabji)

½ small cauliflower cut into small pieces
1 cup shelled peas
1 large potato cubed
1 large tomato chopped
2-3 carrots, diced
2 tablespoons butter
2 cloves garlic chopped fine
½" (1 25 cm) piece of ginger, chopped fine
1 onion chopped fine
1 tablespoon garam masala
1 teaspoon salt
2-3 green chillies chopped fine
Some coriander leaves, chopped fine
½ teaspoon turmeric powder
½ teaspoon cumin seeds crushed
(Many other vegetables also can be used for this recipe)

Heat the butter and add cumin and turmeric and fry for a couple of minutes Add onion, ginger and garlic and brown lightly Add all the vegetables except coriander and green chillies. Stir-fry a couple of minutes and cover to simmer until vegetables are tender. Do not add any water. Remove from the fire, add chillies and coriander and serve in a meal along with meats, yoghurts or breads.

Stir-fried Vegetables (Bhurji)

Bhurjis are vegetables cooked without addition of water. It could be a combination of vegetables or a single vegetable. The best way to use all nutrients in fresh vegetables is to make a bhurji. Garlic and ginger are optional when cooking in the form of bhurji. A good combination for bhurji is cauliflower and potatoes.

A Few Suggested Combinations

Cauliflower, Potatoes and Peas

Cabbage (shredded) and Potatoes
Peas and Potatoes
Spinach and Potatoes OR Spinach and Onions
Capsicums and Eggplant with or without Potatoes
Turnips, Carrots, Peas and Potatoes
Any of the large variety of green beans and Potatoes.
Any of the large variety of leafy greens available
Potatoes with Carrots

Bhurjis should be cooked a little before serving and are usually good with some hot pepper as they are accompaniments to other curries or main dishes. Bhurjis can be cooked with or without onion. Tempered with just a few mustard seeds, celery seeds or cumin seeds popped in hot oil also makes a good dish.

Sauted Turnips (Sukka Shalgum)

1 1b turnips
1 teaspoon salt
1 tablespoon brown sugar
1 teaspoon turmeric
1 tablespoon ghee or oil
2 cloves garlic
½″ piece ginger, chopped fine
2 chopped green chillies or ½ teaspoon chillie powder
1 teaspoon garam masala

Wash, peel and slice the turnips not bigger chan ¾″ (2 cms).
Heat 1 tablespoon ghee, add turmeric, sugar and pieces of
turnips and cook on low fire until tender Keep aside. Heat 1
tablespoon ghee and fry garlic and ginger to a golden brown
colour Add to the turnips with garam masala and mash coarsely.
Cook until no moisture remains. Serve garnished with coriander
leaves. A great favourite with Makki di Roti and lassi or diluted
buttermilk.

Zucchini (Tori)

2 cloves garlic
1 large onion chopped fine
1 lb (450 gm) zucchini
1 large tomato
1 large potato
2 tablespoons ghee or oil
1 teaspoon garam masala
1 teaspoon turmeric
Some coriander leaves chopped fine
Salt to taste

Wash, scrape and cut the zucchini into ½″ (1.25 cms) slices.
Wash, peel and cut each potato into 8 pieces. Heat the ghee, add
turmeric, onion and garlic. Fry to a golden brown and add salt,
zucchini and potatoes. Cook on slow fire until tender. Add
tomato, chopped fine, and garam masala. Stir for a few minutes.
Sprinkle coriander leaves and serve with plain rice or phulka.
To make this vegetable dish more colourful you could add
chopped (½ cup) red sweet pepper or green pepper when adding
the tomatoes

Vegetable Marrow (Ghia)

Could be prepared in the same manner as above

Carrots, Peas and Potatoes (Gajar, Matar or Alu)

1 cup carrots washed, scraped and sliced thinly
1 cup peas (shelled)
1 large potato, cut into 8-10 pieces
1 onion chopped fine

2-4 cloves garlic
½″ (1.25 cms) piece of ginger } chopped fine (optional)
2 tablespoons ghee or oil
1 teaspoon chillie powder
1 teaspoon turmeric
1 teaspoon cumin seeds
1 teaspoon garam masala
Salt to taste

Heat the ghee or oil, add cumin until it pops. Add turmeric, carrots, peas, potatoes, salt, garam masala and chillie powder. Mix well and cook over low heat for 15-20 minutes. Do not add water. Shake the pan to prevent from sticking at the bottom.

Potato Curry (Alu Tariwale)

4 cups water
4 large potatoes
1 teaspoon cumin
1 teaspoon turmeric
1 tablespoon ghee or oil
1 teaspoon amchur
1 teaspoon salt
1 teaspoon garam masala
2 green chillies, chopped fine
Some coriander leaves, chopped fine.

Wash, peel and cut the potatoes into 8 pieces each. Heat the oil or ghee and add cumin, turmeric and potato pieces. Fry for a few minutes and then add water and salt and allow to cook until potatoes are tender and the gravy is reduced to half. Add garam masala, amchur, green chillies and coriander. Remove from the fire and serve with puris or parathas for brunch or breakfast.

Dry Potatoes (Sukke alu)

4 large potatoes
1 teaspoon garam masala
1 tablespoon oil or ghee
1 teaspoon amchur
2-3 chopped green chillies
1 teaspoon turmeric
Some chopped coriander leaves,
Salt to taste

Boil, peel and cut potatoes into 8 pieces each Heat ghee or oil and add cumin, turmeric, salt, garam masala and potatoes. Stir briskly (take care not to break the potato pieces) for 5-7 minutes. Sprinkle coriander and chillies and serve with puris or parathas for breakfast.

Yam Curried (Arbi Tariwali)

1 lb arbi (Yam)
2 medium onions, sliced fine
1 tablespoon oil or ghee
1 teaspoon garam masala
1 teaspoon cumin seeds
½ teaspoon celery seeds
2-4 cloves garlic
1 teaspoon chillie powder
1 teaspoon amchur
1 teaspoon turmeric
Salt to taste
A few coriander leaves chopped fine
1 cup yoghurt
2 cups water

Boil the arbi, not too soft. Remove the skin and cut into strips like french fries or slice into round thick pieces Heat ghee and add celery, cumin, turmeric, until the seeds pop. Add the onions and fry until golden brown. Add arbi pieces, chillie powder, crushed garlic and amchur and stir until arbi is coated or until it starts sticking to the bottom of the pot. Add the yoghurt and mix well. Add water, scraping the bottom of the pot and allow to simmer until the water content is reduced to half Add garam masala, chopped green coriander and serve with rice dishes, or plain phulkas or parathas.

Yam Fried (Sukki arbi)

1 lb (450 gm) arbi
1 teaspoon cumin seeds crushed coarsely
1 teaspoon celery seeds
2 tablespoons oil or ghee
1 tablespoon garam masala
1 teaspoon amchur

1 teaspoon turmeric
1 teaspoon chillie powder
Salt to taste.

Boil, peel and cut the arbi to desired shape and size. Heat the ghee and add celery, cumin and turmeric until the seeds pop. Add the arbi pieces, salt, amchur and garam masala. Fry briskly until all the masalas are coated on to the arbi; the colour is golden brown and pieces fairly crisp. Serve with yoghurt dishes or as an appetizer before meals.

The same recipe can be used for boiled potatoes.

Potatoes in Yoghurt (Dahiwale Alu)

1 lb (450 gm) new potatoes
2 cups yoghurt
2 cups water
2 tablespoons ghee or oil
1 teaspoon turmeric powder
1 teaspoon cumin seeds crushed
1 teaspoon chillie powder
2 green chillies chopped fine
Some coriander leaves chopped fine
1 teaspoon garam masala
1 teaspoon coriander powder
Salt to taste.

Wash, soft boil, peel and cut each potato into 2 pieces. Heat the ghee, add cumin and turmeric. Add the potatoes, garam masala, coriander powder, salt, chillie powder, yoghurt and green chillies. Stir briskly for a few minutes, then add water and allow to simmer until the gravy thickens and reduced to half. Add coriander leaves and serve with puris or parathas for breakfast or brunch.

Tomato Curry (Tamatar Tariwala)

1 lb (450 gm) tomatoes chopped
1″ piece ginger chopped fine
4 cloves garlic chopped fine
1 onion chopped fine
1 teaspoon turmeric

1 teaspoon coriander seeds powdered
½ teaspoon garam masala
3-4 green chillies chopped fine
2 tablespoons oil or ghee
1 teaspoon salt
1 tablespoon sugar (brown)
1″ (2.5 cm) piece cinnamon stick
1 big cardamom
1 bay leaf
A few chopped coriander leaves.

Heat the oil or ghee and fry the onion, ginger and garlic until light yellow. Add the turmeric, coriander powder, chillies, garam masala, bay leaf, cardamom, cinnamon, tomatoes, salt and sugar. Stir thoroughly, cook on low heat until well blended texture is obtained. Remove from the fire. Garnish with chopped coriander leaves and serve with plain rice.

Fenugreek and Potatoes (Methi Alu)

½ lb (225 gm) potatoes
1 lb (450 gm) fresh fenugreek leaves chopped fine
2 tablespoons oil or ghee
1 teaspoons salt
3-4 green chillies chopped fine

Peel and cut potatoes into bite sized pieces. Heat the ghee, add fenugreek and stir-fry briskly for 2 minutes. Add salt and potato pieces and allow to cook covered until potatoes are soft. Add chopped chillies and keep stirring until almost allm oisture evaporates. Remove from the fire and serve with yoghurt dishes and plain phulka.

Watercress or spinach can also be substituted for fenugreek. Spinach-Alu tastes delicious with sour-cream or yoghurt.

Vegetable Koftas

Vegetable Koftas are vegetables mashed or grated, spiced, mixed with a binding agent and formed into balls, the size of a ping-pong ball. The balls are deep fried and cooked in a curry sauce like vegetable curry masala. Vegetable koftas can be prepared with:

grated zucchini and chopped onion
grated marrow and chopped onion
grated potato and shredded cabbage
boiled, mashed potatoes and cauliflower
chopped spinach and mashed, boiled potatoes

All the above combinations have to be mixed with spices and besan (as a binding agent) before they can be fried. Potato Bondas, from the snack section, can also be cooked in a vegetable curry masala to form a kofta curry. Any of the above combinations can be stuffed with a little panir or cottage cheese justl ike stuffed meat koftas. I will give only one recipe as an example.

Zucchini or Marrow Kofta

1 lb (450 gm) marrow or zucchini, grated
1 teaspoon salt
1 cup water
1 teaspoon garam masala
1 cup besan (chickpea flour)
1 onion chopped
2-3 green chillies
1 teaspoon coriander seeds, roasted and crushed
1 tablespoon ghee
1 tomato
1 teaspoon chillie powder
4 cups water or 1 cup vegetable juice + 2 cups water
1 teaspoon salt.

Scrape and grate the marrow or zucchini. Add to 1 cup boiling salted water and boil until the water dries up and vegetable is tender. If the vegetable becomes tender and there is still water you can cool the vegetable, squeeze out the water, and keep it aside for use in the curry. Add green chillies, garam masala and coriander powder. Mix well with besan and form into balls. Fry on medium heat until brown. Keep aside.

Heat 1 tablespoon ghee. Take 2 tablespoons of the prepared vegetable curry masala and stir in 1 teaspoon red chillie powder and tomatoes. Stir until tomatoes are soft and blended with the curry masala. Add water and/or vegetable juice and simmer for ½ hour on low fire. Add the fried koftas and allow to cook until the koftas swell and become soft. At this stage you could also cook in a hot oven for 15-20 minutes. Remove from the fire and serve garnished with coriander greens, onion rings or slices as an accompaniment to plain rice or phulka.

Variations in the preparation of kofta curries can also be made by adding strips of capsicum, boiled or frozen peas, french fried potato scoops or balls, mushrooms, hardboiled whole eggs or pineapple and any other combination you can imagine. You could find a combination that suits your taste by experimenting only.

PULSES

The finest source of protein for a vegetarian is pulses called dal in Punjabi. It holds a particularly important place in every-day food. It is a part of the daily meal of the rich as well as the poor. Their wide appeal proves that they are delicious. There are many varieties of dals grown and eaten in India. There are also as many different ways in which they are cooked. Some of the dals most commonly used in Punjab are:

Moong Dalli (split with husk)	Urad Dalli (split without
Moong Dhuli (split without	husk) Urad Dhuli (split
husk)	with husk)
Moong Sabat	Urad Sabat
Masoor Sabat	Moth Sabat
Masoor Dhuli	Harvan
Channa Dal	Rajmaah (kidney beans).

There are several varieties of the kidney beans and almost all are used as an integral part of a Punjabi meal. Well cooked urad sabat or maah sabat, as it is called, is a delicacy of the Punjab that has yet to find a competitor in any other dish elsewhere. It has the flavour, taste, colour which appeals to almost everyone. The traditional way of cooking it takes a long time (sometimes about 6-8 hours). The dal is cleaned, washed and cooked in a pot with a tight fitting lid. The cooking takes about 6-8 hours and on its completion, is removed from the fire and a 'tarka' or baghar' is added before serving with phulka or slice. Since the task takes so long, I recommend the use of either a slow cooker or, if in a hurry, a pressure cooker.

Black Gram (Urad Sabat)

For the Dal:
1 cup urad sabat
1 teaspoon salt
1″ piece ginger chopped fine
8 cloves of garlic chopped fine or crushed
1 large onion chopped fine
10 cups water
½ teaspoon red chilled powder
½ tablespoon ghee

For Tarka:
2 tablespoons ghee
1 medium size onion
½ teaspoon garam masala
½ teaspoon cumin seeds
½″ piece ginger chopped fine
2-3 green chillies chopped.

Clean, wash and boil the dal in 10 cups of water. When boiling add salt, garlic, ginger, red chillies onion, and ghee. Cover and pressure cook for ½ hour. Then let the pressure drop by itself. Uncover and allow to simmer on low fire while you prepare the tarka.

Tarka

Heat the ghee, add ginger, chopped onion, garam masala, cumin seeds and fry till light brown. Add green chillies to the simmering dal. Cook another ½ hour or until a thick consistency is reached. Serve hot with yoghurt and plain rice or parathas or phulka.

Moong sabat or masoor sabat can be prepared in much the same way, only that a little less water and a little less time is required. Use 8 cups of water and 20 minutes cooking time is sufficient. They can be garnished with chopped coriander leaves.

Split Green Gram or Lentils (Moong Dhuli or Masoor Dhuli)

1 cup masoor or moong dhuli dal
½ teaspoon turmeric
¼ teaspoon chillie powder or paprika

½ teaspoon cumin seeds
2 cloves garlic crushed
2 green chillies chopped fine
Some coriander leaves
2½ cups water
1 tablespoon ghee.
½ teaspoon salt
½ teaspoon black pepper.

Clean and wash the dal and pressure cook for 5 minutes with turmeric, salt, chillie powder, crushed garlic and water. Allow pressure to drop. In the meantime heat the ghee, add cumin seeds and green chillies. Fry for two minutes and add to the dal. Add chopped coriander greens and serve with phulka, rice or as a soup with juice of ½ lemon squeezed in it.

Chickpeas, Potato Curry (Alu Chollae Taridar)

1 cup chickpeas
1 teaspoon salt
½ teaspoon turmeric
2 tablespoons ghee
1″ piece ginger
1 large onion crushed
6 cloves garlic crushed
2 large tomatoes or 1 cup tomato juice
10 cups water
1 teaspoon garam masala
1 teaspoon amchur
1 teaspoon chillie powder or paprika
1 large potato
½ cup yoghurt
Some corriander leaves chopped fine

Clean, wash and soak chickpeas in 10 cups of water with 1 teaspoon salt, overnight. The next day boil until tender. Strain and keep water and chickpeas separately. Heat the ghee, add garlic and onion paste and stir briskly until it becomes light brown. Add the turmeric, cumin, chillies and garam masala and mix well with chopped tomatoes and cook until a smooth consistency is obtained. Peel and cut each potato into 8 pieces. Add the potato pieces and chickpeas to the onion paste and cook for a few minutes. Then add the water strained from chickpeas and cook until only a little gravy remains or until the potatoes are tender. Add the beaten yoghurt and mix well. Cook for 5 minutes and add amchur and coriander. Serve with rice, nan, phulka or bhatura.

Fried Urad Dal (Sukki Dal)

1 cup urad dal dhuli
1 tablespoon ghee
½ teaspoon salt
½ teaspoon turmeric
¼ teaspoon black pepper
2 big cardamoms
1″ piece cinnamon
1 teaspoon cumin seeds
1 large onion sliced thinly
Some chopped coriander leaves

Clean, wash and cook the dal in 5 cups of water. Add turmeric and salt. When tender strain and keep aside. Heat the ghee. Add cumin until it pops then add cardamom and cinnamon and stir for a couple of minutes. Add the onion and cook until golden brown Add the boiled dal and black pepper, being careful not to break the grains of dal. Stir in coriander leaves and serve with a vegetable curry, yoghurt dish and phulka, puri or nan. The appearance is similar to fried rice.

You could use the same recipe for channa dal also, except add fenugreek leaves instead of coriander which imparts a particularly good taste.

Kidney Beans (Rajmaah)

1 cup kidney beans
1 large onion chopped fine or grated
2 large tomatoes chopped
2 green chillies chopped
4-6 cloves garlic crushed
½ teaspoon cumin seeds
1 teaspoon garam masala
Salt and pepper to taste
2 tablespoons ghee

Some chopped coriander leaves
4 cups water or stock
1 teaspoon paprika
1 teaspoon turmeric

Clean, wash and soak rajmaah overnight. Add the salt and boil until tender. Separate from water and keep aside. Do not throw away the water; use as stock for the curry.

Grate or grind together onion and garlic. Mix in paprika. Heat the ghee and fry cumin seeds for a couple of minutes, then add the onion paste and stir-fry briskly until brown. Add turmeric, pepper and chopped tomatoes and cook until tomatoes are tender and the paste is smooth. Add the boiled rajmaah and cook for 5 minutes taking care it does not settle at the bottom of the pan. Add 4 cups water or stock. It could be a little more or less and will not make much difference. Cook until it resembles a thick stew. Add garam masala, coriander and green chillies. Beat the yoghurt thoroughly and add to the curry stirring well. Remove from the fire and serve hot with plain rice, phulka or by itself.

For variety, the same recipe can be used with hamburger meat, stirfried and mixed in with the Rajmaah when the onion paste is ready. The salt and garam masala will have to be doubled in quantity.

Tinned kidney beans can be cooked in the same way.

There are also a lot of varieties of beans like lupen beans, moth, black-eyed peas, pigeon peas; they can all be cooked in the same manner.

Lentils and Spinach (Dal Saag)

1 cup moong or masoor dal
1 lb spinach chopped fine
3 cups water
1 medium onion, chopped
1 teaspoon cumin seeds
½ teaspoon turmeric
1 teaspoon garam masala
2 tablespoons ghee
½ teaspoon chillies or 2-3 green chillies
Salt to taste (very little)
½" piece ginger crushed

Clean and wash the dal and boil with water, salt, chillies and turmeric. Cook for 10 minutes, then add finely chopped spinach. Cook on moderate heat until the moisture dries up. In the meantime, heat ghee and add cumin seeds. After a while add the onion and ginger and fry until golden brown. Stir into the dal with garam masala. Cook for another 5-7 minutes taking care it does not stick to the bottom of the pan. Serve hot with a knob of butter and plain phulka.

Kabli Channa (Chollae)

½ cup tomato juice
1½ cup chickpeas
10 cups water
½ teaspoon bicarbonate of soda
1 teaspoon salt
1 teaspoon cumin seeds
2 large onions sliced
4 cloves garlic
2 tablespoons ghee
1" piece ginger, cut into thin strips
2 large tomatoes sliced
1 lemon cut into wedges
1 tablespoon garam masala
1 teaspoon chillie powder
2 large black cardamoms
1" piece of cinnamon
1 teaspoon ground coriander
Some coriander leaves, chopped fine
2 tea bags

Clean, wash and soak the chickpeas and tea bags in 10 cups of water. Discard the tea bags, add salt, cardamoms, cinnamon and bicarbonate of soda and boil gently on slow fire until peas are tender but whole and the water is absorbed Heat the ghee, add cumin seeds until they pop and then add garam masala, coriander powder, chillie powder and chopped garlic and mix briskly. Add the boiled chickpeas and blend together being careful not to mash the chickpeas. Add tomato juice and take out into a serving dish. Leave in a moderately hot oven (350°F) for ½ hour.

Serve in a shallow dish in a heap or pyramid. Garnish with sliced green chillies, ginger, sliced onion, tomatoes, wedges of lemon and coriander leaves. It can be served warm or cold, with tamarind chutney, phulka, bhatura, rice or nan. Cooked this way it turns out delicious and is also convenient to prepare when having a lot of guests.

The same recipe can be used for kala channa (black chickpees), pigeon peas, lobia beans, rongi beans and several varieties of beans.

This recipe can also be tried in the oven after all the masalas have been added. However, it must be kept in mind that not as much moisture is required when baking.

Urad Channa Dal (Maah Chollae di Dal)

1 cup urad dal (split, husked or unhusked)
½ cup channa dal
4 cups water
½ teaspoon turmeric
½ teaspoon black pepper
½ teaspoon salt
2 whole red chillies
2 teaspoons ghee
1 teaspoon cumin seeds, crushed
1″ piece ginger, chopped fine
Few fresh coriander leaves chopped
1 onion chopped fine
2 cloves garlic chopped fine

Clean, wash and boil both the dals in 4 cups of water. Add turmeric, salt, black pepper and chillies, and cook until tender and blended well with the reduced water. The combination of these two dals brings out a very pleasant flavour and coarse texture. Heat the ghee, add cumin, ginger, onion, and garlic. Brisk fry until onions are golden brown. Pour this over the cooked dal and mix well. Serve garnished with coriander leaves as one item of a meal. It is particularly liked served with tundoori roti, parathas or rice.

Channa Dal With Marrow

1 cup channa dal
2 cloves garlic + 1 onion, chopped or sliced
4 cups water

½ lb marrow (vegetable) cut into 2" squares
½ teaspoon garam masala
2 tablespoons ghee
Salt and pepper to taste
½ teaspoon turmeric
1 teaspoon chillie powder
Coriander leaves chopped
1 green chillie chopped

Clean, wash and soak the dal for a couple of hours in 4 cups
of water. Add salt, turmeric, chillie powder and boil. When
boiling, bring down the temperature and simmer on low heat
until grains are nearly tender. Add the pieces of marrow and continue to simmer until the marrow is soft and the dal well blended
with water. If you find the gravy too thick add some more boiled
water as sometimes the marrow may need extra water and time
to soften. Take off the heat and keep aside. Heat the ghee and
fry the onion, garlic and ginger until a golden brown. Add the
chopped green chillies and pour this tarka over the dal and mix
well. Garnish with coriander leaves and serve as an item in any
meal. Caution must be observed not to let the marrow pieces
get over-cooked as the pieces whole and tender floating in the
dal give a very colourful effect and a delicate, subtle flavour.

It must be noted that in the Punjab no vegetable is normally
added to the dal. When coriander leaves are not available during some months of the year it is equally good to use dried
fenugreek (methi) leaves. Add them about 5 minutes before
removing the dal from the fire. The flavour of dried and crushed
fenugreek leaves in dal is irresistible.

7 Non-Vegetarian

The mosaic of religions and cultures, make India a treasure-house of meat and fish dishes. Many in India eat meat on special occasions. The Muslims do not eat pork and the Hindus and Sikhs, do not eat beef. It has not always been so because early Sanskrit writings indicate that meat and game was commonly eaten. In some of the recipes given here, beef or veal can be substituted for mutton or lamb. Meat, poultry ānd fish are expensive in India and therefore cooked mainly for parties and on festive occasions.

Meat, in north America and Europe, is usually tender and does not require long cooking as it does in India. Therefore, I have modified the recipes accordingly. The time taken for cooking is also determined by the condition the meat is in i.e., frozen or fresh. Frozen chicken gives quite good results but I prefer to cook fresh young chicken.

Lean beef and chicken mince is also easier to cook. It can be served with plain chapati, rice, spaghetti or with bread.

In Punjabi homes if meat is tough it is either rubbed with a piece of green papaya or marinated or cooked in a Tandoor. Tandoori chicken is, perhaps, one of the most delicious and relished all over the world. A tandoor is a clay oven and the process of cooking in it is very close to grilling. It is wide and cylindrical, closed at the bottom. It comes in different sizes. It is from the top that firewood is shoved in; when the tandoor is really hot and the flames subside food is put in it for cooking Tandoori roti is a speciality of Punjab. It is flattened and stuck to the wall of the tandoor with moistened hands, and is a skill by itself. There are several recipes for making tandoori chicken and these vary from family to family But a couple of fundamentals are the same The chicken should be young and small. It should be skinned and marinated so as to soak in all the various flavours and juices so necessary to produce a moist yet dry roast like meat. Instead of a tandoor, a rotisserie, barbecue or trivet in the kitchen oven will also do as a substitute.

Ingredients for Marinating Tandoori Chicken
(for one chicken about 1½ lb. in weight)

4-6 cloves garlic
1 small onion grated.
1" piece ginger (more or less as desired)
1 cup yoghurt
1 teaspoon garam masala
1 teaspoon salt
1 lemon, extract juice
1 teaspoon chilli powder (hot)
A pinch or two of red food colouring (optional)
½ teaspoon cumin seeds, ground.
½ cup ghee, if cooking in the oven
Cooking time 1-1½ hour

METHOD I

Clean, wash and dry chicken and make a few cuts on the thighs and breast. Rub with salt and lemon juice and keep aside for half an hour In the meantime grind all the ingredients except yoghurt, food colouring and ghee. Make a paste with yoghurt and rub on the chicken making sure to insert into the cuts on the thighs and breast. Leave aside, covered, for at least 4-6 hours or overnight in the fridge. Grease a baking pan and place the chicken on it, breast down, removing the excess paste. Spoon half of the ghee on the chicken and cook on moderate heat (325°F). Baste occasionally with the left over marinade. Halfway through the cooking brush with ghee and the food colouring and turn the chicken over, breast upwards and repeat the process, basting occasionally. Lastly, place under the grill for 5 minutes. This gives the chicken a nice brown colour.

The use of a rotisserie gives good results. If cooking on a barbecue, put the chicken on a rack above the fire, turn occasionally to ensure it cooks all around. Do not prick the chicken when cooking. Serve with a tossed salad or rice, phulka or nan.

METHOD II

Clean and wash the chicken. Rub the marinade paste thoroughly inside and outside and place the chicken on a trivet. Add 1 cup water and pressure cook for 10 minutes. When pressure drops add the ghee and cook without the lid till the water evaporates. Add the colouring and sprinkle with finely chopped green chillies, coriander leaves or fenugreek leaves and leave to grill in the oven for 10 minutes. Serve hot with rice, pulao, phulka or nan.

METHOD III

A sauce can be prepared by cooking tomatoes in 2 table-spoons of butter, 1 teaspoon sugar, and ½ teaspoon salt. Strain through a sieve and add 2 tablespoons of cream or yoghurt. Keep aside until required.

Prepare with marinade as for method I and gently cut the chicken into pieces In a dutch oven, on the stove, fry the pieces of chicken on moderate heat in butter or ghee. When broken slightly add the yoghurt mixture kept aside and cook, stirring gently and occasionally until the sauce penetrates and dries up. Remove from the heat and sprinkle with cumin seed powder, and coriander or parsley greens chopped fine. Serve with rice, phulka, nan or any other kind of plain bread or on a platter with salad around the chicken. All the above methods can be tried with either whole chicken or chicken pieces.

Chicken with Spinach (Palak Murga)

1 chicken (1½-2 lb)
4 cloves garlic
2 medium size tomatoes
2 oz. (50 gm) spinach
2-3 green chillies
1 tablespoon garam masala
Salt to taste
2 teaspoons sour cream
2 tablespoons butter
Oil or ghee for frying.

Clean, wash and cut the chicken into desired sized pieces. Fry to a golden brown and keep aside Slice and chop spinach, onions and grind the rest of the ingredients except oil, butter and sour cream. Heat the butter or ghee and fry onions until light brown. Add the ground paste of garlic, garam masala, salt and tomato and cook for 10 minutes on low heat. Add the spinach and cook for 10 minutes before adding some cream. Arrange chicken pieces in a pan. Cover tightly and cook on low heat until chicken is tender. Serve with phulka or plain boiled rice

Chicken Curry

Masala paste:

1 chicken 1½-2 lbs	4 tablespoons ghee
2 large onions	Coriander leaves
4-6 cloves garlic	4 green chillies
1″ piece ginger	½ cup yoghurt
1 tablespoon garam masala	½ cup water
8 oz tin of pineapple with its syrup	1 teaspoon turmeric
1 teaspoon cumin seeds	6-8 peppercorns
1 teaspoon coriander seeds	Chillies or paprika.

Grind or blend onions, garlic and ginger in half the ghee. Roast cumin, coriander and peppercorns and grind to a fine powder. Add the onion mixture and stir-fry for 5-8 minutes, add turmeric also. Brown the chicken pieces evenly in the remaining ghee. Remove and add to the onion and masala paste and mix thoroughly. Add ½ cup water, ½ cup yoghurt and pineapple and either cook on the top of a stove with tightly fitting cover or cook in a moderate oven for about 3/4-1 hour with lid on. Remove when done and sprinkle with chopped coriander and green chillies.

Fried Chicken

1 chicken, about 2 lbs (900 gm)
½ cup all-purpose flour
1 teaspoon salt
1 teaspoon paprika
½ teaspoon cumin seeds
½ teaspoon coriander seeds
½ teaspoon garam masala
½ cup cream or yoghurt
1½ cups breadcrumbs or crushed cornflakes
Oil for frying

Wash, clean, skin and cut the chicken into pieces. Mix flour, breadcrumbs or cornflakes, salt, cumin seeds, coriander seeds, garam masala and paprika and keep aside in a plastic bag. Dip the chicken pieces in cream or yoghurt and then roll in the breadcrumbs or cornflakes mixture. Fry in hot oil for a few minutes and turn the pieces over so as to cook and brown evenly on all sides. Put fried chicken in a covered roasting pan and leave in a moderately hot oven for 10-15 minutes and serve with salad or a rice preparation.

Instead of frying, the same procedure can also be adapted for cooking in the oven in a heavy roasting pan or tray. It uses up less fat when done in the oven, because only about 2 tablespoons of oil is necessary to coat the roasting pan. Chicken wings can also be prepared this way.

Honey Garlic Chicken

I learnt to cook chicken this way in Malaysia.

1 chicken (about 2 lbs)
4-6 cloves garlic crushed
1 medium onion sliced
1 tablespoon grated fresh ginger
2 tablespoons soya sauce
2 tablespoons ketchup
½ cup honey
1 teaspoon salt
1 teaspoon garam masala
1 lemon juice, extracted
4 tablespoons cooking oil

Wash, clean, skin and cut chicken into small bite sized pieces. Heat the honey, ketchup, soya sauce, salt, garlic, onion and garam masala for a few minutes and add the cooking oil. Pour into a shallow baking tray with chicken pieces and bake for about 45 minutes or until tender and done. Alternately, cook over a stove adding ½ cup water.

Chicken with Pineapple

Prepare the chicken as for Honey Garlic Chicken. Roll the pieces soaked in the marinade of honey mixture into breadcrumbs and roast in an oven for 45 minutes with 1 lb unsweetened pineapple pieces. Serve with a salad or rice

Curried Partridge (Curried Titar)

6 partridges or any other game bird (about 1 lb.)
1 large tomato
1 teaspoon turmeric
4 tablespoons ghee
2 large onions chopped fine
$\frac{1}{2}$" piece ginger chopped
4 cloves garlic chopped fine
$\frac{1}{2}$ teaspoon black pepper
$\frac{1}{2}$ teaspoon chillie powder or paprika
2 large black cardamoms
6 cloves
1" stick cinnamon
1 teaspoon cumin seeds
3 tablespoons yoghurt
1 teaspoon coriander seeds
1 cup water
Salt to taste
$\frac{1}{2}$ cup lemon juice.

Clean, wash and dry birds, sprinkle with lemon juice and salt both inside and outside. Finely chop the giblets and keep aside. Fry chopped onion, garlic and ginger; add turmeric. Roast cardamom, cinnamon, cloves, cumin and coriander seeds and grind with black pepper and tomato to make a paste. Add to the onion mixture and giblets and fry for a few minutes. Mix in the yoghurt.

Smear this paste over the birds and also stuff inside; leave to marinate for 8-10 hours or leave covered in fridge overnight. Remove the excess paste and roast the birds in a moderate oven, 350°F, for about 45 minutes, sprinkled with paprika or chillie powder. Baste occasionally until the birds are done The one cup water can be added and the birds can be cooked with the marinate over the stove in a dutch oven (big patila). Sprinkle with coriander leaves and serve hot with nan, phulka or rice.

The same recipe can be used for roasting a duck either whole or on the stove top in a dutch oven by cutting into pieces.

Be careful to use enough oil. Serve hot with boiled peas, carrots and baked potatoes.

Mincemeat (Sukka Keema)

½ cup tomato juice or vegetable juice
1 lb. lean mince beef or chuck (chicken mincemeat)
1 large onion
2 large tomatoes
4 cloves garlic
½″ piece ginger
1 teaspoon turmeric
½ teaspoon garam masala
½ teaspoon chillie powder or paprika
½ teaspoon ground coriander seeds
½ teaspoon cumin seeds ground
1 cup peas (shelled)
2 tablespoons oil or ghee

Chop the onion and garlic fine. Fry until onions become transparent. Add grated ginger, chopped tomatoes and turmeric. Add the mince and fry until dry and brown (about 20 minutes). Add the spices, peas, salt and ½ cup tomato juice and simmer for 15 minutes or until liquid is absorbed and the meat is tender. Drain off any excess oil and serve with plain boiled rice or phulka. If using fresh peas make sure you add them when the onions are ready. The leftover can be used the next day by cooking in a spaghetti sauce and served with boiled spaghetti or rice.

Meat Balls Curried (Kofta curry)

1 lb. (450 gm) mincemeat (beef, lamb or mutton)
1 large onion, chopped fine
6 cloves garlic crushed
1″ (2.5 cm) piece ginger grated
2 tablespoons chickpea flour or
1 slice of bread or 1 egg
1 teaspoon garam masala
Some coriander leaves and 4 green chillies
1 teaspoon cumin seeds crushed
1 teaspoon salt
Ghee or oil for frying

Mix thoroughly the mince, onion, garlic, ginger, spices, coriander, green chillies, and either 2 tablespoons chickpea flour or 1 egg or 1 slice of bread soaked in milk for 10 minutes. Knead the mixture thoroughly and form into balls firmly, about 1½ (4 cm.) in diameter and deep fry to a golden brown colour. Fry gently, remove balls carefully and keep aside. These koftas can be eaten with cocktails or at tea parties and can also be served with a curry or sauce prepared thus:

Gravy or Sauce for Meat Balls (Koftas or Kababs)

2 tablespoons ghee
1 teaspoon turmeric
1 teaspoon coriander crushed
1 large onion grated or chopped
4 cloves garlic, crushed
1 tablespoon garam masala
½ (1.25 cm) piece ginger
2 large tomatoes
1 cup yoghurt
1 cup water
1 teaspoon salt
Some coriander leaves finely chopped
1 teaspoon chillie powder (optional)

Heat the ghee and fry onions and garlic until brown. Add the turmeric, spices, and salt and stir for a few minutes. Add the sliced or chopped tomatoes and cook until the tomatoes and onion mixture is blended in thoroughly. Add the yoghurt and allow to simmer for a few minutes. Add the fried koftas and simmer on gentle heat taking care not to handle too much, lest the koftas fall apart. When the koftas look swollen, add the coriander leaves and put into a dish to serve with plain rice, pulao, nan or phulka.

I must mention here that this recipe can be modified thus:

For Stuffed Balls or Koftas

2 full boiled eggs
½ cup chopped pistachio nuts
½ cup chopped, blanched almonds
½ cup raisins (kishmish)

Salt to taste
1 teaspoon black pepper.

Chop full boiled eggs and add raisins, pistachios, salt and pepper. When forming the koftas into firm balls, punch with the thumb and put into it 1 spoon of the filling. Use a little water to help form the koftas into round balls or even flat rounds like cutlets or patties. Deep fry to a golden brown colour. Can be served as it is or cooked in the sauce as above.

Sheekh Kabab (Meat Kabab)

1 lb (450 gm) minced beef, mutton, lamb or goat
1 large onion chopped fine
4 cloves garlic crushed
1 (2.5 cm.) piece ginger grated or crushed
2 tablespoons besan (chickpea flour)
1 egg
1 teaspoon poppy seeds
½ lemon, juice extracted
1 tablespoon garam masala
½ teaspoon coriander seeds crushed
½ teaspoon cumin seeds crushed
15 almonds ground (2 tablespoons.)
1 teaspoon chillie powder or paprika
4 tablespoons ghee
10 peppercorns
1 tablespoon salt
4 green chillies chopped
A few coriander leaves chopped.

Roast the poppy seeds, almonds, cumin, coriander seeds and peppercorns. Grind and mix with ginger, besan, egg, lemon juice, salt and garam masala. Mix into the mince and add red chillie powder or paprika. Knead well adding a few drops of water or buttermilk (lassi) if necessary to make a sticky, pliable paste suitable to cover the skewers, or seekhs as they are called in India. Add the chopped coriander and green chillies and press the meat paste on the greased skewers in the shape of sausages Use a moist hand when shaping and firmly press the meat on the skewer. Roast in an oven at 350°F or on the barbecue. Turn the skewers slowly and gently so that the paste does not fall off. Baste with oil occasionally and when brown and done, gently slide off the skewers and serve hot with onion salad and mint or coriander chutney or sauce.

The same mixture can also be shaped into a sausage over flat wooden toothpicks and shallow fried. These can be used with a curry sauce like koftas or kababs and served with rice.

Shallow Fried Cutlet (Shammi Kabab)

Prepare the stuffing as stated for stuffed koftas. Using the seekh kabab meat paste, divide into 16 or 18 portions. Place a spoonful of the stuffing on one portion of the meat paste and tightly pack with moist hands. Flatten out a bit and shallow fry on medium heat. When well browned serve with onion rings, salad or mint chutnney.

Kidney Curry (Gurda Curry)

1" (2.5 cm) piece ginger grated
1 lb (450 gm) kidneys (lamb)
2 large onions chopped or sliced
2 cloves garlic crushed
3 large tomatoes chopped
1 teaspoon turmeric
1 teaspoon cumin seeds crushed
1 teaspoon coriander seeds ground
½ teaspoon garam masala
2 bay leaves
Salt to taste
Coriander leaves, chopped
2 tablespoons oil or ghee

Wash and cut the kidneys to bite size. Fry the onions until golden brown, add garlic, ginger, tomatoes, spices and salt and stir-fry for 10-15 minutes. Add the kidneys and cook on moderate heat until tender. Add coriander leaves and serve with plain roti, or plain rice, and kuchumber salad (onion and tomato salad).

Hussaini Seekh Kabab Curry

Liver pieces can be cooked in the same way. Fried pieces of lamb, mutton, or stewing beef on wooden skewers roasted

with tomato and green peppers can be served at cocktail
parties and/or cooked in a curry as for kofta curry.

For the kabab:
1 lb (450 gm) meat cut into 1″ cubes
8-10 skewers or flat toothpicks
10-12 small onions peeled
8-10 pieces of ginger cut into ½″ cubes
1 green pepper cut into 1″ cubes or larger
1 large tomato

For the marinade:
1 large onion grated
1 teaspoon coriander powder
1 teaspoon cumin powder
1 teaspoon poppy seeds roasted
4 tablespoons oil or ghee
4 cloves garlic crushed
1 teaspoon turmeric
1 teaspoon garam masala
1 cup yoghurt
1 teaspoon red chillies
1 teaspoon salt

Grind all the ingredients of the marinade into a fine paste and
soak the meat pieces in it for about 4 hours or keep covered
overnight in the fridge. Remove the meat from the marinade and
arrange on the wooden skewers alternately with tiny button
onions, thin slices of ginger and green pepper cubes. Do not
keep any piece close to the edge. Heat ghee and fry skewers
in a shallow pan until lightly browned. Remove from the ghee
and keep aside.

Prepare the curry as for kofta curry and allow skewers to
be cooked in it gently and until a thick gravy remains. Serve
with rice, roti or nan.

Fish Preparations (Machhi)

Fish preparations are popular in the North but only in some
families and eaten occasionally. Usually pomfret (a sea-fish) and
bangra, prepared like tandoori chicken, are popular. Sometimes prawns are cooked in a curry.

Fish has a smell very peculiar to it. In order to get rid

of the fishy smell you should soak it in a solution of vinegar, tamarind or lemon juice and salt. I prefer to remove the fishy smell with a paste of 1 teaspoon turmeric, 1 tablespoon salt, 2 tablespoons of chickpea flour, mixed with a little water and rubbed over the fish. After about 2 hours hold the fish and wash under cold water and the smell will have gone. It is a good idea to cook fish enough to render it tender to eat; do not overcook as the flavour will be lost.

Fried Fish

1 lb (450 gm) pomfret or 2 large bangra (herrings)
Salt to taste
1 large onion grated
2 cloves garlic crushed
½ teaspoon turmeric powder
½ teaspoon garam masala
½ teaspoon chillie powder or paprika
½ lemon, juice extracted
1 tablespoon coarsely crushed coriander seeds
Chopped coriander leaves
2 green chillies chopped
Oil for frying
2 tablespoons yoghurt
2 tablespoons besan (chickpea flour)

Prepare and wash the fish, sprinkle with salt and keep aside. Mix thoroughly the onion, garlic, turmeric, garam masala, coriander, lemon juice, chillies, coriander leaves and besan with the yoghurt into a paste. Spread this paste outside and inside of the fish and fry in oil on both sides until golden brown. Serve hot with onion salad and lemon wedges.

Prawn Curry (Jhinga Curry)

4 cloves garlic crushed
1 lb (450 gm) prawns peeled and deveined
1 large onion chopped
1″ (2.5 cm.) piece ginger grated
2 green chillies chopped fine
Salt to taste
2 tablespoons yoghurt

1 teaspoon turmeric
1 teaspoon cumin seeds crushed
4 bay leaves
1 teaspoon garam masala
½ teaspoon paprika or chillie powder
4 tablespoon ghee

Heat the ghee and add spices, onion, garlic and ginger. Stir-fry until the mixture is golden brown. Add the yoghurt and salt and cook for 5-10 minutes until a smooth consistency is formed. Stir in the prepared and washed prawns. Cook for about 5-10 minutes stirring gently. Add some water and simmer for 15 minutes or until the prawns are tender. Serve hot with plain rice or roti and onion salad.

8 Sweetmeats and Desserts

Sweetmeats (Mithai)

No Punjabi meal is complete without a dessert or sweet. It is common to serve the sweetmeat before a meal at large wedding parties and festivals. The sweets are served on religious functions also, among family and friends present on the occasions.

Pheniya

This delicate vermicelli like stuff, sold in close clusters or rounds by the weight or by the piece, is prepared by boiling in milk and adding sugar to taste. While boiling the milk one crushed cardamon could be thrown in for flavour or a few drops of rosewater are sprinkled. The consistency usually varies according to the individual taste. A few minutes boiling in the milk is all that is required. These are delicious served hot or cold.

Bread Pudding

8 slices bread
2 eggs
½ cup sugar
¼ cup raisins
1½ cup milk
1½ tablespoons butter
1 tablespoon coconut shredded
½ teaspoon vanilla essence

Boil the milk with sugar and allow to cool. Beat the eggs and mix with the milk and essence. Lightly toast the bread and butter it sparingly. While arranging in a loaf pan sprinkle a few raisins between the slices of bread and pour over the milk. Sprinkle almonds on top and bake in moderate oven, 300°-325°F, for 30-45 minutes or until the pudding is set. Test the pudding with a wet knife. If it comes out clean then it is cooked. Sprinkle coconut and leave in the oven for another 2 minutes. Serve hot.

Instead of raisins you could use mixed dried fruit chopped and soaked in brandy.

Macaroons

3 egg whites
2 cups sugar
3 cups desiccated coconut
½ cup almonds slivered
2 drops vanilla essence

Heat the oven to 325°F. Beat the white of eggs stiff or until it stands in peaks. Continue to beat while adding sugar. Mix in the coconut. Grease a baking tray. Add the vanilla, mix and spoon on a greased tray spacing 1½" away from each other. Sprinkle a few almond slivers on each. Bake for 30-35 minutes or until lightly coloured at the tips. Remove from the oven and allow to cool. Lift off the tray and keep aside. Serve as a snack. Do not store until well cooled.

Dudh Pera

2 cups milk powder
1 can evaporated milk (1½ cups)
1½ cups sugar
3 tablespoons butter or ghee
2 cardamoms ground
10-12 pistachio nuts chopped fine
3-4 strands saffron

Mix the evaporated milk, sugar, saffron and butter. Cook until it thickens. Add the cardamoms and remove from the fire. Add the milk powder a little at a time stirring constantly to avoid forming lumps. Return to the heat and cook 5 more minutes stirring all the time. Remove from the fire and allow to cool until it is comfortable to handle. Quickly make small balls of the entire mixture. Place a few pieces of almonds and pistachios in the centre and press down with your thumb, so that the finished 'pera' looks like a thick round with a hollow decorated with nuts in the centre. If you do not wish to press down with your thumb then the back of a glass should do the job.

Saviya

Saviya is very much like fine Italian vermicelli. It is customarily used by the Muslims at a festival called Id. Using the same recipe good results can be obtained with fine spaghetti or vermicelli or ask for a packet of Saviya at the Indian or Chinese food stores.

5 cups milk
2 tablespoons saviya (about 125 gm)
1½ cups sugar
2 tablespoons raisins
6-8 almonds or pistachio nuts sliced
2 cardamoms, seeds crushed
Sprinkling of kewra or rose water.

Boil the milk, add saviya and cook on moderate heat, stirring occasionally, until the saviya are tender and milk thickened. Add the sugar, cardamom and raisins and cook for about 5 more minutes. Remove from the fire and add kewara or rose water. Serve sprinkled with sliced nuts either cold or hot. The consistency should be like rice pudding or kheer.

Saviya Pulao

1 lb saviya, vermicelli or fine spaghetti
1/2 cup butter or ghee
1 cup water
1 cup dried milk powder
2 cups sugar
1 cup milk
1 tablespoon kewra essence or
Rose water with few strands of saffron soaked in it.
2 small cardamoms
4 cloves
1" piece of cinnamon
½ cup raisins

3-4 silver vark (leaves)
10-12 pistachios
½ cup slivered almonds

Use a shallow wide pan with heavy bottom. Fry the saviya in
ghee and add cinnamon, cardamom and cloves. Stir constantly
until deep brown. Add the water and simmer covered until it
is absorbed. In the meantime, mix together milk and sugar to
a paste. Pour the milk paste over the saviya and cook on very low
fire. Do not stir, only test to see if moisture is absorbed by tilting
the pan sideways. Add kewra or rose saffron, and raisins.
Gently lift with a fork to turn over a little. While turning over
add half the almonds. Turn out like a mound on a serving
tray and garnish with pistachios and almonds. Alternately, bake
in a moderate oven, 350°F, for 5-10 minutes or until the water
is absorbed. Decorate with nuts and silver vark.

Jalebi

For the syrup:
3 cups sugar
3 cups water
Few strands of saffron
1 teaspoon yellow food colouring
2 cloves crushed
2 cardamoms seeds, crushed
Oil for deep frying
For the batter:
Ingredients—I
1½ cups all-purpose flour (maida)
2 tablespoons chickpea flour (besan)
2 tablespoons yoghurt
2 pinches yeast
Hot water.
      Or
Ingredients—II
2 cups self-raising flour
2 tablespoons yoghurt

Mix all the ingredients of either I or II and keep aside for at
least 2 hours. In the meantime prepare the syrup by boiling the
sugar and water to a one thread consistency. Just as it reaches

the one thread consistency add the crushed cloves, cardamoms, saffron and colouring. Keep warm. Heat the oil in a wide shallow pan and squeeze out the batter through a ¼″ wide hole made in a cloth bag or an icing bag, into little circles, or coils (about 2-2½″ diameter) or figure of eight quickly. Turn once to allow both the sides to become crispy golden brown. Remove and soak in warm syrup for a few minutes. Remove from the syrup and arrange in a pyramid form in a serving dish. Decorate with silver paper.

Pancakes (Malpura)
1 cup all-purpose flour (maida)
½ cup semolina (suji)
1 cup sugar
1 tablespoon fennel seeds (saunf) crushed coarsely
2 small cardamoms crushed
½ cup milk (a little less or more)
Oil for frying

Mix all the ingredients thoroughly to make a thick batter and allow to stand for an hour. In a frying pan heat the oil or ghee and pour out a little batter like a pancake into it (these Malpuras are not to be made very thin or very big). The diameter should be roughly 3″-4″. Turn over and fry until done on the second side. The edges will tend to get darker in colour and the centres will remain lighter. This allows you to decorate them with nuts and cream in an attractive manner. A truly delicious menu for a rainy day is Malpura with Kheer (Rice pudding).

1½ cups wholewheat flour can be used instead of 1 cup allpurpose flour and ½ cup semolina to which is added one medium, ripe, mashed banana.

Suji Halwa
1 cup semolina (Suji or wholewheat flour)
1 cup sugar
1 cup butter or ghee
4 cups water
Few strands saffron
2 cardamoms, seeds crushed
10-12 blanched, sliced almonds
A handful of raisins
8-10 finely chopped pistachio nuts

Mix the saffron with a few drops of water and grind. Add to
the sugar and water and boil for a few minutes. Keep aside until
required. Heat the ghee, add the cardamom seeds and suji and
fry to a golden brown colour. Add the syrup and cook until all
the water is absorbed. Mix in briskly the raisins and almonds
and stir for a couple of minutes. Remove from the fire and
serve garnished with pistachio nuts.

It is customary to serve this dish to the congregation at a
Gurudwara (Sikh temple) after the prayers every day. It is called
Prashad and is usually prepared after a morning bath. The
raisins and nuts are excluded and it is prepared with wholewheat flour.

Gulab Jaman

For balls:
2 cups milk powder
1 cup readymade pancake mix (Tea-bisk)
4 tablespoons melted butter
Milk to knead the dough
2 tablespoons granulated sugar

For syrup:
2 cups sugar
2 cups water
1-2 tablespoons milk
2 cardamoms crushed
A few drops rose water
Ghee or oil for deep frying

These are basically made with khoya and panir (soft panir
soft cream cheese). Both these are not easily available so I have
given ingredients that can be obtained from a local grocery
store and the dish prepared is very much the same. However,
in India both are available and can be used to prepare Gulab
Jamans. The recipe using khoya and panir is also given.

For balls

1 cup khoya
2 cups soft panir
2 tablespoons flour (maida)
2 tablespoons fine sugar

Mix the khoya and paneer until they are soft and smooth. Knead in the flour and sugar a little at a time, until all is used up. Keep aside for a while and then knead again till a very soft and smooth dough is obtained. Prepare balls and proceed as given below.

Prepare the syrup with sugar, cardamom and water. When boiling stir in 2 tablespoons of milk. Remove any scum that travels to the side of the dish. Cook for 10-15 minutes and remove from the fire and keep aside.

For the balls mix tea bisk and milk powder. Rub in the butter and knead into a soft, pliable dough with milk, added a little at a time. Keep aside for half an hour or more and shape into small balls, the size of a walnut. Make a depression in the centre and add 2 pinches of sugar and roll the ball to a smooth surface. Heat the ghee and take care to regulate the temperature on medium low. In other words fry the balls on medium heat. Fry these balls gently in ghee to a deep brown colour evenly. Remove with a slotted spoon and allow to soak in cold syrup for 2 hours. Return the syrup with the balls to heat and allow to simmer till the balls swell but do not crack. A little water should be added if the syrup thickens.

Rasagulla

Rasagullas are white soft balls of panir floating in a flavoured syrup.

For balls:
2 cups soft panir (refer to Introduction for its method of preparation)
1 tablespoon flour
1 pinch baking powder.

For syrup:
2 cups sugar
6 cups water
Few drops rose water or kewra essence.

Knead the panir with hands well until all grains disappear and a smooth soft consistency is obtained. Add the flour and baking powder, kneading in well. Divide the mixture into small balls (walnut size) and shape them smoothly. Keep aside, while you prepare the syrup.

Boil the sugar and water for 10-15 minutes. Lower the heat, add the cheese balls gently and let them simmer for 30 minutes or until the balls become spongy and soft. If the syrup tends to thicken sprinkle some water. Adding a teaspoon of water at a time occasionally thins the syrup as well as allows the balls of cheese to get porous and soft. When they are done they settle down at the bottom in the syrup. Remove from the fire; allow to cool and soak for a few hours. Serve cold sprinkled with rose water.

Chickpea Fudge (Besan Pinni or Burfi)

2 cups sugar
1 cup chickpea flour (besan)
1 cup semolina (sooji)
2 cups butter
2 cups almonds
1 tin condensed milk (8 oz.)
1 oz. fresh milk
2 cardamoms crushed
1 cup raisins (optional)
2 cups milk powder

Soak the almonds overnight. Remove the skin and blend to a paste with condensed milk and some fresh milk. Keep aside until required. Heat the butter, stir-fry the besan and sooji until light brown. Add cardamoms and sugar and briskly fry for a few minutes, being careful not to allow the sugar to caramalize. Add the raisns and almond paste, stir constantly taking care that it does not stick to the bottom. Remove from the fire and spread on a tray. Pat the mixture with greased hands and keep aside to set and cool. Cut with a sharp knife into squares or diamonds. Serve with tea or breakfast with milk. To make pinni do not set in a tray. Take a tablespoon of the besan and roll into balls with hands while still warm. It will not be easy to bind together if it gets cold.

Panjeri

2 cups semolina (sooji)
2 cups sugar
2 cups butter or ghee
1 cup raisins

1 cup slivered almonds
3-4 cardamoms (elachi)
2 cups milk powder
1 tablespoon ginger powder (optional)
1 tablespoon celery seeds—roasted and ground (optional).

Heat the butter or ghee and fry the sooji briskly till golden brown. Add raisins, almonds, cardamoms, ginger and celery seeds. Fry for 5 minutes. Add the sugar and mix in the milk powder thoroughly. Remove from the fire and cool before storing in an airtight container. Serve as a snack. A little more butter and few more spices (javitri, jaiphal) can be added if desired.

It is usually taken by the mother of the newly born.

Fudge (Burfi)

2 cups panir or Ricotte cheese
2 cups sugar
3-4 cardamoms (small, crushed)
1/2 cup butter
3 cups milk powder
1 teaspoon essence or rose water.

Heat the butter and cook panir on low fire until all lumps are broken. Add the sugar and cardamoms and cook, stirring constantly until the sugar melts and all water evaporates. Mix in briskly all the milk powder. Add essence and mix thoroughly. Remove from the fire and set in a plate or tray. When cool cut into desired shapes with a sharp knife. Remove gently and serve as a snack.

Decorate with silver paper, shredded coconut or nuts. A few drops of green or yellow colouring can be added to give a pleasing effect. Raisins or nuts can be ground to a paste and added along with the milk powder. It is a favourite of children and adults alike. Keeps well in the fridge for a week.

Carrot Halwa (Gajrela)

2 lbs (1 kilo) carrots grated
2 cups sugar
3-4 cardamoms
4-6 cups milk

1 cup condensed milk
2 cups milk powder
1 cup slivered almonds
1/2 cup raisins
I lb. (1/2 kilo) butter or ghee
2 sheets silver paper (varak) optional

Cook the grated carrots in milk until tender and the milk evaporates. Add cardamoms, almonds, sugar, butter and cook till all the moisture dries up. Add raisins, condensed milk and milk powder. Stir briskly and remove from the heat. Cool and store in an airtight canister in the fridge or spread in a tray and cut into large chunks as for fudge. Decorate with silver paper before cutting into pieces. A little shredded coconut mixed with it gives it a good taste.

Pumpkin Halwa (Kaddu Halwa)

2 lbs (1 kilo) pumpkin
1½ cups sugar
3-4 cardamoms
1 cup slivered almonds
½ cup raisins
1 cup butter or ghee
1 cup milk
2 tablespoon rosewater.

Cut, remove seeds and peel the pumpkin. Chop into small pieces or slices, wash and place on slow fire to cook with sugar, milk and ghee. Cook until soft. Add cardamoms and slivered almonds and stir constantly until all the moisture evaporates. Add raisins and rosewater; mix thoroughly and remove from the fire. Serve garnished with silver paper or shredded coconut. Good as a snack with a glass of milk or as a dessert with cream or custard.

Peanut Toffee or Fudge (Moomphali Gachak)

2 cups roasted peanuts (skins removed)
2 cups jaggery (gur)
1 tablespoon ghee or oil

Heat the ghee or oil and add jaggery. Cook till 1½ thread consistency is obtained, stirring constantly. Add peanuts, stir briskly and pour over a greased surface or tray. As it cools it will harden. Either cut into desired shapes when slightly cool or allow to cool completely and break into small pieces.

It can be prepared with almonds and sesame seeds also to which a teaspoon of celery seeds and/or onion seeds have been added.

Sweet Bread

5 eggs
2 cups milk
2 cups sugar
1 cup butter
2 tablespoons yeast
3-3½ lbs (1½ kilo) flour.(approximately)
6-8 strands saffron.

Soak the saffron in a few drops of water. Prepare the yeast as per instructions on the yeast tin or packet. Mix warm milk and sugar in a large pot. Add 4 beaten eggs and prepared saffron. Mix the yeast, which has now risen and is soft, to the mixture. Start adding the flour, a little at a time, stirring with a spoon until it is ready to knead. Using the melted butter a little at a time, knead the dough well. The butter should all get used up and the dough should be soft and pliable—not too hard. Cover and keep aside until the dough doubles in size. Break out a handful of the dough and using a floured surface gently make into desired shapes or plaits (braids) and leave on a baking tray to rise (2-3 hours). Brush the surface with beaten egg and sprinkle sesame seeds or shredded nuts. Cook in a moderate oven (350° F) for about 45 minutes. Slice when cool or break with fingers to eat. This bread does not require application of butter or margarine.

Sugar Cookies (Nan Khatai)

3½ cups all-purpose flour (maida)
½ cup semolina (sooji)
2 cups sugar
2 eggs
1 teaspoon vanilla essence
½ teaspoon baking powder
1 teaspoon cream of tartar
1 teaspoon nutmeg
2 cups butter

Mix the nutmeg with 2 tablespoons of sugar and keep aside until required. Cream the remaining sugar with butter until well blended, light and fluffy. Mix together the flour, baking powder and cream of tartar and add the creamed mixture. Keep in a cold place (fridge) for about 2 hours or until easy to handle. Place on an ungreased tray with a spoon or shape into small balls and place them on a tray. Flatten with the bottom of a glass dipped in sugar and nutmeg mixture. If the sugar and nutmeg mixture is left over sprinkle it on the cookies and bake for 20 minutes on the middle rack in a moderate oven (325° F). Remove and cool before storing in an airtight container.

9 Snacks

There are a number of snacks both sweet and savoury; they range from the simple titbits to the very complicated ones. Home-made snacks are cheaper than those bought in the market and better in quality as you know what ingredients have gone into their preparation. Tea-time is an important time in India because supper is a late meal. In North America, of course, snacks play an important role as appetisers or with drinks.

Pakoras are the most versatile of snacks, as the batter can be mixed and fried quickly if unexpected guests arrive, and almost any vegetable can be used in its preparation. Pakoras are tastier when served hot but even cold they are a very satisfying dish served as finger foods. Vegetables that can be used are potatoes, onions, spinach, pumpkin, peppers, eggplant, carrots, celery and cauliflower. They can be mixed, chopped or sliced.

Peanut Toffee

1 cup besan
½ cup sooji
2 cups roasted peanuts
125 gm jaggery or boora sugar
2 tablespoons butter
4 tablespoons water

Remove the skins of peanuts. Roast the besan and sooji in butter till lightly brown. Prepare the syrup by mixing jaggery and 4 tablespoons of water until it reaches the thread stage. Add to the roasted flour mixture. Mix the peanuts and stir rapidly till the edges start getting a little bent. Remove from the fire and spread on a greased tray. When set, cut into shapes or break into pieces.

Cheese Toast

1 cup milk
2 tablespoons all-purpose flour
4 slices bread
250 gm cheese
Salt to taste

Make a paste of flour and 2 tablespoons milk. Heat the rest of the milk and slowly add to the flour paste stirring all the time till it thickens. Then add the cheese and salt. Cook slowly till the cheese melts and the mixture is creamy. Spread on slices of bread and grill or toast in an oven. If desired, pepper or mustard can be added to the paste.

Pakora

Basic batter for pakoras

1 cup besan (chickpea flour)
$\frac{1}{2}$ teaspoon salt
$\frac{1}{2}$ teaspoon coriander seeds crushed
$\frac{1}{2}$ teaspoon cumin seeds crushed
1 teaspoon amchur (optional)
1 egg (optional)
1 teaspoon red chillie powder
Ghee or oil for frying

Sift the flour, add salt, coriander, cumin, red chillies and amchur (if using). Mix well with a little water at a time to make a smooth, thick batter. If you want to use egg it must be added along with the water to prepare the batter. Beat thoroughly until the batter is fluffy and creamy. Keep aside for 1 hour or so while you prepare the vegetables. Heat the ghee or oil in wok or karai for deep frying. When hot, drop pieces dipped in batter and fry to a golden brown colour. Remove from the oil, drain and serve either hot or cold with mint chutney, tamarind chutney or tomato ketchup. If using a combination of chopped spinach or mixed vegetables it is convenient to mix in the vegetables with the batter and drop into the hot oil with a tablespoon. It is also good idea to fry a large quantity to a little less brown and fry them a second time when required; they will be crisper and tastier.

Some hints for preparing vegetables for pakoras:

Onion

Peel and slice thickly. Sprinkle a pinch of salt and use as individual pieces to be dipped in the batter, or, chop fine and mix into the batter with hot green or red peppers.

Potatoes

Peel and slice potatoes (about $\frac{1}{4}''$ thick). Soak in cold water to avoid discolouration. Drain and dry thoroughly before immersing in batter.

Spinach

If you are lucky to find fresh leaves wash, drain and pat dry them. Fry coated in the batter individually, cutting off the stems or wash, clean, drain and chop very fine and mix into the batter.

Eggplant

Wash and slice into $\frac{1}{2}''$ thick pieces. Fry each piece dipped in the batter or cut into $\frac{1}{4}''$ cubes along with chopped onion and cubed potato. Mix with the batter and drop into hot oil frying to a golden brown colour. Another suggested good combination is to mix garlic salt, amchur and ground coriander seeds in equal quantities, rub it on to the sliced eggplant and set aside for a few minutes before immersing in batter.

Capsicums (Simla Mirch)

Wash and slice into $\frac{1}{2}''$ thick pieces or strips. Remove seeds and mix into the batter or discard them.

Chillie Pepper

Wash and drain. Slit lengthwise, being careful not to cut them into two. Make a paste of equal quantities of anardana, yoghurt, garlic salt and cumin seeds. Stuff into the chillies and keep aside for a few hours to dry out. Dip into the batter and fry till crisp golden brown. Served with dal it is a very pleasing accompaniment.

Cauliflower (Gobi)

Wash and cut into flowerettes of medium size. If large, slice the flowerettes or break the flowerettes and boil them for five minutes in salted water. Drain and dry on a kitchen cloth. Make a masala of equal quantities of amchur, cumin seeds, celery

seeds and garlic salt. Sprinkle on the boiled flowerettes and allow
to infuse for a few minutes before dipping into the batter to fry.

Panir

Cut panir into 1½″ cubes. Make a masala of equal quantities of ground cumin seeds, amchur and garlic salt. Slit the
panir pieces and sprinkle into each some of this masala. Roll the
panir cubes gently into this masala also. Keep for a few
minutes before dipping into batter to fry. Do not leave them in
the batter for a long time because the pieces will break and will
not fry well and become too hard.

Pumpkin

Prepare in the same way as for potatoes, or you could shred
and chop a combination like (1) spinach, onions, potatoes and
peppers; (2) cauliflower, green onion and potatoes with coriander greens; (3) chopped green onions, peppers and garlic; and
(4) panir pieces.

As you fry pakoras you will notice a little batter splutters
and separates from the pakoras. This must be removed as you
go along. These small pieces can be used with tamarind chutney,
by themselves, or to make boondi or pakori raita. It is delicious
used as a sprinkle on salads or soups.

Potato Bondas

1 cup besan batter
2 large boiled potatoes
2 green chillies chopped fine
Some coriander leaves chopped fine
¼ teaspoon red chillies
½ teaspoon garam masala
Oil to fry
Juice of one lemon and salt to taste

Mash the potatoes and mix in all other ingredients. Form
into balls, dip into the pakora batter and deep fry to a golden
brown colour. Serve hot with any chutney.

Dal Pakora

2 cups urad or moong dal (split)
1 tablespoon salt

1 teaspoon chillie powder
1″ piece of ginger grated
Some coriander leaves chopped fine
2-3 green chillies chopped fine
1 teaspoon cumin seed powder
½ cup water
Oil to fry.

Clean, wash and soak the dal overnight in water. Drain and blend with ½ cup water, ginger, chillie powder, cumin seeds and salt, or pulverize on a grinding stone. Turn out into a bowl and add coriander leaves and green chillies. Beat well for a few minutes until the paste is light and fluffy. Drop a tablespoonful into the hot oil and fry to a golden brown. Remove with a slotted spoon and serve hot or cold, with chutney.

Potato Tikkie (Alu Tikkie)

For the tikkie (Crust):
1 lb potatoes
½ teaspoon garam masala
½ teaspoon salt
½ teaspoon chillie powder
2 slices bread (wholewheat)

For the stuffing:
½ cup channa dal
2 cups water
1 teaspoon cummin seed powder
1″ piece ginger grated
½ teaspoon salt
2-3 green chillies chopped fine
Some coriander leaves chopped fine
Oil for shallow fat frying.

Crust

Boil, peel and mash the potatoes. Add garam masala, chillie powder and salt. Mix thoroughly. Soak the slices of bread in water for a minute and squeeze them well. Add to the potatoes and mix well. Keep aside.

Stuffing

Cook the dal with salt and water until soft and moisture is

soaked up. Mash with fingers or a fork Mix in cumin, ginger, chillie and coriander. Mash the dal coarsely.

Take a little of the potato mixture for a tikkie and flatten out on the palm Place a teaspoonful of the stuffing in the centre and fold up the potato mix. Roll on the palm gently and flatten out taking care that the stuffing is not visible. Shallow fry in a heavy bottomed frying pan. Handle gently so that the tikkies do not break. Fry crisp to a deep golden brown colour and serve with chutney or relish or a yoghurt preparation. These tikkies can be served in buns like a hamburger also.

Vegetable Cutlets

1 large boiled potato
1 small onion chopped fine
½ cup boiled green peas
½ cup boiled green beans
1-2 medium size yams boiled
1 teaspoon salt
1 teaspoon garam masala
1 teaspoon cumin seed powder
3-4 green chillies chopped fine
Some coriander leaves chopped fine
½ cup breadcrumbs
2 slices bread (wholewheat preferred)
4 cloves garlic
Oil for shallow frying

Mash the potato, yam, peas and beans. Add salt, onion, garlic, cumin, chillies, garam masala, coriander and mix well. Soak the bread in cold water for a minute and squeeze it. Mix thoroughly with the vegetable mixture. Spread out a tablespoon of the paste and shape on the palm into either a round or oval and shallow fry after lightly coating with breadcrumbs, to a golden brown colour. Serve as a snack with a salad or chutney.

Channa Dal Cutlets

2 cups channa dal
1 large onion chopped
2-3 green chillies chopped fine
Some coriander leaves chopped fine

1 teaspoon salt
½ teaspoon red chillie powder or paprika
Ghee or oil for deep frying

Pick, wash and soak the dal overnight. Drain and grind to a stiff paste: a blender is not very suitable for this purpose; a '*sil vatta*' must be used. Mix in chillies, coriander, salt and onion. Flatten out one tablespoon of this paste on a greased palm and shape either round or oval, into ¾'' thickness or shape into balls the size of a ping-pong ball and deep fry on low heat to a golden brown colour. Heat the oil or ghee on high heat and then bring down the temperature when cutlets are added. Remove when done and drain. Slit and through the width carefully spread a little chutney (mint, coriander, coconut or tomato) inside without breaking it. Serve as a snack.

Fruit Chat

All fruits and vegetables in season can be used to prepare chat. A great favourite as a snack or an appetizer, the combination of vegetables and fruits depends on the individual taste.

Prepare a masala with equal quantities of roasted cumin seeds, roasted coriander and amchur (mango powder). Add a pinch or two of black salt and black pepper or chillie pepper and keep in a bottle for use as required.

Fruits suitable for chat

Sweet potatoes	Peaches, Plums
Boiled potatoes	Pineapple fresh or tinned
Sliced tomato	(if tinned drain all syrup)
Cucumber cubed	Orange wedged
Banana sliced	Kiwi fruit peeled and sliced
Apples diced	All kinds of berries
Peas boiled	Raspberries, Loganberries
Strawberries sliced	Grapes seeded
Lemon juice	

Mix fruits and/or vegetables, as desired. Sprinkle with some of the above mentioned masala. Mix well and squeeze some lemon juice over it. Chill before serving. A little yoghurt and some tamarind chutney can also be added. Do not add yoghurt and chutney in the bowl. Individuals can spoon on to their own helping, if required. Garnish with raisins and nuts.

Besan Sev or Gathia

2 cups besan (chickpea flour)
2 tablespoons ghee or oil
½ teaspoon cumin seeds ground
½ teaspoon ajwain (celery seeds) ground
½ teaspoon chillie powder (optional)
½ cup water
Salt to taste
Oil or ghee for deep frying
A potato masher can be used to pass the sev dough through

Sieve the besan, add 2 tablespoons oil or ghee and rub well. Add cumin, celery, chillie powders, and salt. Mix into a stiff dough. A pinch of turmeric can be added if a slightly yellow colour is desired. Heat the ghee or oil for deep frying. Put the dough into a vermicelli or sev machine (as it is called). Hold the machine a few inches above the oil and pass the dough through to fall into the hot ghee or oil, swiftly moving your hands in a rotating motion so that the sev do not fall into one place. Fry till golden crisp. Remove, drain and break them a bit. Cool and store in airtight containers. Serve as a snack. Tamarind chutney, well beaten yoghurt, pakories raita can be served with sev.

Papries

½ cup fine semolina
½ cup all-purpose flour (maida)
1 teaspoon melted ghee or oil
¼ cup cold water
Salt to taste.
Oil or ghee for deep frying.

Sieve the flour and add salt. Mix 1 teaspoon melted ghee. Make a stiff dough with cold water and knead the dough well for 10-15 minutes. Keep it aside for 1 hour. Roll out the dough very thin using oil and not flour for dredging the board or rolling pin. Cut into rounds about 1½″ in diameter. Prick with a fork and crisp fry to a light golden brown colour on low fire. Remove, drain the oil and serve with chat or as an appetizer in the following manner:

Take 1 cup well beaten yoghurt and 1 cup tamarind chutney in separate bowls. Soak for few minutes, some papries in chutney and some in yoghurt. Arrange alternately in individual serving plates or shallow bowls. Sprinkle the masala, mentioned earlier, in fruit chat. Serve with mint chutney, chopped, boiled, diced potatoes and chopped green chillies. It is convenient to leave all the food in bowls on the table and allow the guests to help themselves to it as they wish.

Mathi

5 cups all-purpose flour (maida)
1 cup melted oil or ghee
1 teaspoon salt
1 teaspoon celery seeds (ajwain)
1 teaspoon cumin seeds (jeera)
½ teaspoon dill seeds crushed
10-12 peppercorns whole (optional)
Oil or ghee for deep frying

Sieve the flour and salt together. Add cumin, celery and dill seeds and mix. Put 1 cup melted oil or ghee and knead well into a stiff dough, using cold water. Turn out on to a board and roll thinly. Cut into rounds about 3″ in diameter and press a peppercorn in the centre; or roll out thinly and cut into diamond shapes, squares, triangles or strips, as desired. Heat the oil and fry until crisp and lightly brown on slow fire. Drain and cool before storing in an airtight container. Keeps well indefinitely.

Mathis are also made in very large sizes (8" in diameter) on the occasion of a marriage or religious ceremony. In Punjab it is a tradition to distribute Mathis and shakkarparras among friends and relatives. This tradition was observed to announce the wedding date.

Shakkarparra

6 cups flour (maida)
Milk to knead the dough

1 cup melted butter, ghee or oil
4 cups sugar
2 cups water for syrup
8-10 cardamoms crushed
2-3 cloves powdered or crushed
Oil for deep frying.

Sieve the flour and rub in melted ghee. Knead into a stiff
dough with the milk. Keep it aside for about an hour. Knead
well again and divide into 4 balls. Roll out one ball at a time
into $\frac{1}{2}''$ thickness. With a sharp knife cut out the rolled dough
into $\frac{1}{2}''$ cubes or diamonds. Heat the oil for deep frying and
gently put in the cubes and fry over medium heat, stirring once
or twice until golden and crisp. Remove from the oil with a slotted spoon and keep aside. Proceed in the same way with the other
3 balls of the dough. Keep Shakkarparras aside in a large bowl.

Prepare the syrup with sugar and water to which cardamoms
and cloves are added. Cook until one and half thread consistency is reached. Remove from the fire and pour over the fried
cubes and stir briskly for a few minutes until the syrup starts
to dry on the 'parras' or golden fried cubes. Cool and store in
an airtight container. Keeps well for about a month or so.

Gangas

The same dough as for 'Shakkarparras' could be rolled out
into thin rounds about $3-3\frac{1}{2}''$ in diameter. Make 3-4 slits in the
centre taking care not to separate the strips at the edges. Lift
from the rolling board and hold edges and twist together firmly.
Deep fry on moderate heat to golden crisp and keep aside.
Make the syrup to 1 thread consistency and dip the gangas in the
syrup for a couple of minutes. Take out and place on a serving
dish. Decorate with sliced almonds or pistachio nuts when it is
still moist. These will dry as the sugar crystallises on cooling.
Cool and store in an airtight container. Serve as a snack.

Stuffed Gangas

Dough same as for shakkarparras
1 cup semolina roasted in $\frac{1}{2}$ cup butter
$\frac{1}{2}$ cup sugar

1½ cups mixed chopped nuts and
raisins (cashew, almonds, pistachios).

Oil for frying

Divide the dough into walnut sized balls. Roll out into thin rounds about 2-2½″ each. Alternately roll out into a large round. Cut several pieces 2-2½″ in diameter. Place 1 tablespoon stuffing on each piece. Cover with another round and secure edges by moistening with water. Heat the oil and fry a few at a time until brown. Remove and dip in the syrup. Serve as a snack. It is advisable to have two persons working together when making gangas.

Curried Mixed Nuts

2 cups cashews raw
2 cups almonds (blanched or whole)
2 cups peacams or walnuts
2 tablespoons garam masala
1 teaspoons salt
4 tablespoons melted butter or ghee

Mix all the ingredients and spread in a roasting tray or a shallow pan. Bake in a moderate oven for 15-20 minutes, shaking once or twice, to infuse the flavouring of spices. When done, remove, cool and store in an airtight container taking out a little at a time as required.

Sweet and Spicy Nuts

1 cup honey or 2 cups brown sugar +½ cup water
1 cardamom crushed
½ teaspoon cinnamon powder
A pinch of clove powder
1 tablespoon grated orange or lemon peel
6 cups mixed raw nuts (cashews, almonds, walnuts etc.)
1 teaspoon salt

Mix all the ingredients and cook in a heavy bottomed shallow pan or 'Karahi', or wok until the nuts are coated well and the skin starts to make a crackling sound. Do not undercook. Sugar should turn into one thread consistency so that the nuts will get well-coated and shiny. Remove from the fire, cool and store in an airtight container, in the fridge if necessary.

Samosa

Vegetable stuffing

    2 large boiled potatoes
    ½ cup green peas (either boiled or frozen)
    1 teaspoon salt
    1 teaspoon garam masala
    2 green chillies chopped
    Some coriander leaves chopped
    ½" piece ginger grated (optional)
    1 tablespoon ghee or butter.

Cut the boiled potatoes into fine cubes. Heat the ghee and add peas, spices, salt and potatoes. Mix and cook, stirring constantly, until all the ingredients are well mixed. Remove from the fire and mix in green chillies and coriander. Keep aside.

Pastry or covering

    2 cups maida
    3 tablespoons ghee or oil
    ½ teaspoon salt

Mix together 2 cups maida, ½ teaspoon salt and 3 tablespoons of melted ghee. Knead into a stiff and smooth dough with plain yoghurt or buttermilk. Keep aside for ½ hour and knead again with oil or ghee smeared on hands. Divide into lime-sized balls and roll outin to smooth, even and thin circles. Cut each circle into halves and proceed as follows.

Lift a half circle on your left palm and moisten the edges. Make a cone and fill it with a spoonful of the prepared stuffing. Press the moistened edges to close the cone firmly. Deep fry on moderate heat until crisp and golden brown. Serve with any green chutney or tamarind chutney. The samosas should all be prepared and kept covered with a moist towel. Fry a few at a time.

The samosas can be prepared and fried a day before any party. Cool and store in a canister or plastic bag in the fridge. Just before the party they can be heated in an oven for 20-25 minutes and served as an appetizer with a yoghurt preparation, chollae or chutney.

Mincemeat or mincemeat and peas can be prepared and used as a stuffing. The puff pastry mix available in the store can be used as samosa covering.

Khatai

3 cups all-purpose flour
½ cup semolina (cream of wheat, suji)
1 cup butter (at room temperature)
1 cup sugar
½ teaspoon baking powder
1 egg
2-3 small ground cardamoms (elachi)
4-6 slivered almonds.

Cream the sugar and butter until light and add the semolina, egg, baking powder and flour. Knead into a crumbly dough. Add a few spoons of water, if needed, to prepare the dough. Place spoonfuls on a greased tray. Put a littles slivered almonds and ground cardamom on each and press down slightly with fingers and bake in a moderate oven (300-325°F) for 35-40 minutes or until light golden. Do not over-brown them. Cool and store in an airtight container. Keeps well for long periods.

10 Drinks and Beverages

Drinks are an important part of the meal. This is more true of Punjab in view of extremes of climate and the hard work the people do. Drinks are usually served as refresheners, and also as household remedies for minor ailments. Fresh fruit juice is the best and in the West with all the appliances in the kitchen it is not a bothersome process either. The fruits available in India are varied, its climate, languages and weather. India has all the common like the West—apples, pears, apricots, plums and peaches and besides, it also has malta, jamun, phalsa, leechee, mulberry (shatut) chickoo, sugarcane, mangoes and melons. Next to fruits and juice, yoghurt and milk based drinks are relished the most.

Plain Buttermilk (Lassi)

1 cup plain yoghurt
2-3 cups water
Salt and pepper to taste (optional)
1 pinch of cumin seeds, roasted and crushed

Blend together the yoghurt and water and pour over ice in large glasses. Mix salt, cumin and pepper, if desired, or leave plain and drink any time or with meals specially with Saag and Makki di Roti.

Sweet Butter milk (Meethi Lassi)

1 cup yoghurt
2-3 cups water
A pinch of nutmeg
2 tablespoons sugar
½ teaspoon rose-water or kewra essence

In a blender mix the yoghurt, water and sugar until frothy.
Or pour from one jug to another several times and with a little
force till froth is formed. Sprinkle rose-water or kewra essence
and nutmeg. Pour over ice into large glasses and serve as a
cooling drink in hot weather.

Lemonade (Shikanjavi)

Juice of 2 lemons
2 glasses water
2 tablespoons sugar
A pinch of salt
Ice

Dissolve sugar in water. Add the lemon juice and mix thoroughly. Pour over ice and serve in tall glasses as a thirst quencher.

Milk Shake

Banana :

1 ripe banana
1 tablespoon sugar
2 glasses milk
A pinch of nutmeg
½ teaspoon rose-water
Ice

Peel and cut the banana into milk. Add the sugar and blend
on high speed for a couple of minutes. Sprinkle rose-water and
serve with ice and nutmeg sprinkled or stirred into it.

Mango

1 ripe mango
1 tablespoon sugar
2 glasses milk
Ice (optional)
A pinch of nutmeg or
½ teaspoon rose-water

Wash and peel the mango. Slice the pulp and add it to
milk. Add sugar and blend on high speed for 2 minutes. Serve

poured on ice in a tall glass, sprinkled with nutmeg or rose-
water if desired.

Milk Soda

½ cup milk
8 oz or 1 can orange coke or club soda
1 teaspoon sugar

Dissolve the sugar in milk and pour over ice in a large glass.
Pour club soda or orange coke on top and serve as a thirst
quencher.

Almond Milk (Badamwala Doodh)

10-12 almonds
2 glasses milk
1 cardamom crushed
1 tablespoon sugar
2 drops rose-water

Soak the almonds overnight. Peel, grind and mix with the
milk and sugar Boil until well blended. Add cardamom and
remove from the fire. Serve hot or cold poured over ice with
rose-water, as a cool milk shake.

Spiced Milk (Masalewala Doodh)

1 glass milk
1 cardamom
1″ stick cinnamon
1 clove
½ tablespoon sugar
4-5 ground almonds or cashewnuts

Boil the milk, spices and nuts for a few minutes. Remove
from the heat and take out spices. Dissolve sugar and serve
piping hot on a cold day.

Shardhai

This is a cold, nourishing, spicy and thirst quenching drink
consisting of a lot of seeds, nuts and spices mixed with milk.
The proportions could be varied according to taste.

½ cup almonds
12-14 pistachio nuts
½ cup mixed ⎧pumpkin seeds
magaz   ⎪cantaloup seeds
                    ⎨melon seeds
                    ⎪gourd seeds
                    ⎩cucumber seeds
2 tablespoons khaskhas (poppy seeds)
2 cups sugar
6 cardamoms, crushed
1 tablespoon white peppercorns
½ cup fennel (saunf)
6 cups water
1 cup milk

Soak the nuts overnight. Separately soak magaz, saunf and khaskhas. Drain, peel the nuts, add peppercorns and cardamom and put into blender, or grind on a grinding stone or in kundi danda and liquefy with the 6 cups of water. Strain through a cheesecloth. Mix milk the and sugar and serve chilled. A few rose petals (dried) could be used when blending all the ingredients to give flavouring.

Spiced Tea (Masalewali Chai)

1 tablespoon sugar or to taste
2 cups water
2 cups milk
1 tablespoon tea leaves
2 cardamoms
½" piece cinnamon stick
1 clove
½ teaspoon fennel seeds

Add the spices to water and boil for a few minutes. Add tea leaves and milk. Allow it to boil for a minute and lastly add sugar. Remove from the fire and set aside for a couple of minutes. Strain and serve.

Carrot and Beetroot Spicy Drink (Kanji)

4 small carrots   ½ teaspoon mustard seeds (black) crushed
1 small beetroot   ½ teaspoon chillie powder

1 (64 oz) empty jan

1 tablespoon salt
½ teaspoon ajwain (celery)

Wash, scrape and cut the carrots into strips. Wash, peel and slice the beetroot thickly. Put in the jar and add crushed clelery, mustard seeds, chillie powder and salt. Fill to the top with water and secure lid tightly. Keep in a sunny place for 8-10 days before serving as a cool drink poured over ice.

Sugarcane Juice (Ganne da Ras)

This is usually available in wayside stores in India when the sugarcane season arrives. It is quite impossible to obtain the sugarcane juice in North America as we seldom get fresh sugarcane and none of the kitchen appliances are suitable for extracting its juice Canned juice, however, is available and can be used.

Grind 2″ piece ginger with a little water and strain. Mix in the juice of 1 lemon. Add to 2 cups of sugarcane juice (canned) and pour from one glass to another glass with force until well mixed and frothy. Add salt to taste and serve chilled.

11 Preservation of Food

Preservation of food has been in vogue from the earliest times as foods in their natural state remain in good condition only for a short while. Pre-historic man preserved his vegetables and fruits by drying, milk in the form of cheese and refined or clarified butter (ghee) and fruit juices in the form of wines. When man started to hunt he also began to dry or salt his meat and fish. It has now become so commercialised to preserve foods that new methods and processes have been developed and are changing the way of life depending on the needs of the individual. Pickling, salting, smoking and drying of foods had been practised by our ancestors for centuries. Cold storage, freezing, canning and chemical preservation are some of the methods now used. Convenience, quality and economy are important factors in processing foods for preservation. The modern objective of food preservation is more than just preventing spoilage.

Drying and dehydration are nature's own methods of preservation. Drying usually means drying foods in the sun and dehydration means removing the water-content of food even though it may be by artificial means. During the World Wars I and II dehydrated foods were of great utility and since the end of World War II efforts have been made in all countries to improve the quality of dehydrated foods. Considerable activity in the field of research and development has resulted in improved quality and research is still on for better and faster methods.

Sun-drying is used for fruits and fish all over the world. In olden days and even now, in India and many other lands, the method of drying in the shade is used for foods such as fenugreek (methi) greens, coriander greens, green onions, garlic, mustard greens, cauliflowers, herbs, mint, turnips, chillies and mushrooms. According to whether the foods are available only part of the year, the method used is to store a good supply to last the family for the rest of the year.

Pickling in India is usually done in oil; in the Punjab mainly in mustard oil. Pickling process depends on the presence of salt or an acid substance (like vinegar) or both. Vegetables used for pickling are usually high in water content and this water has to be removed. Salt solution is more concentrated than the vegetable and thus some of the water is taken out of the vegetable to equalize the concentration of salt in the entire quantity. To bring out a clear pickle the *vegetables* are stuffed in jars and covered with spiced vinegar liquid In mustard pickle the vegetables are mixed with a combination of spices, vinegar or oil whatever the need may be. *Chutneys* are cooked slowly or blended in a blender or pulverized in a mortar wit hpestle (Kundi ghotna) to a smooth jam-like consistency. In pickles the chunks of vegetables are kept to a recognizable shape of the true vegetable whereas in chutneys and sauces they are cooked or ground to a smooth pulp. Pickles, chutneys, sauces, jeilies and jams do not have a high nutritive value. They are used mainly for adding variety and taste to the meals.

Syrups: Sugar is added to pure fruit juice or pulped and strained whole fruit or berries using the minimum amount of water. Tightly closed bottles are then placed in the hot sun or chemical preservatives are added. Citrus fruits and berries are very suitable for making syrups.

Candied fruits are obtained by cooking either big chunks of fruit or whole fruit in a syrup until it is clear and soft. You should start with a light syrup of sugar and water and as the fruit cooks, add more sugar gradually to thicken the syrup; this avoids the toughening of the fruit in the process Do not handle too much with spoon or fork but when the appearance seems to tell you that the fruit is ready and plump to look at, drain the thick syrup and slowly allow the fruit to dry or quickly cook further to crystallize on high heat. Sliced ginger is one such item used in abundance and goes well with dried fruits and nuts.

Murabba (Fruit Preserve) are jams and jellies made from fruits that are acidic hence the product is sterile. The high sugar content and sourness of the acidic fruit is the basis for preservation of jams and jellies. Marmalades consist of fruit slices and peels of various citrus fruits suspended in jelly. Conserves and preserves are whole or large chunks of fruit.

PICKLES, CHUTNEYS AND FRUIT PRESERVES
(Achar, Chutneys and Murabba)

A meal In India is never complete without pickles and chutneys which form a necessary and important accompaniment to a meal. Pickles and chutneys stimulate the appetite and promote digestion. It is not impossible these days to make a classic Indian preserve, chutney or pickle here in the West where all the ingredients are available; only that the sun is not as hot and as bright as you need for the slow processing it takes to produce a perfect pickle. The recipes of pickles are really a very closely gaurded secret in a family and are handed down from generation to generation. The main ingredient in most pickles is a combination of various spices—crushed or powdered. Some vegetables are best alone in a mustard base with vinegar and some in oil. In Punjab mustard oil is commonly used for pickles When preparing pickles the mustard oil is heated to smoking stage and then kept aside for use as called for in each recipe.

The standard pickles are made with mango and lime but almost any vegetable can be pickled. There are several varieties of chutneys and fruit preserves that a Punjabi housewife makes.

There are chutneys which do not require any cooking. They are perishable and are prepared fresh every time. The mature chutneys take time for the ageing process before they can be eaten. And then, of course, are the pickles that require lengthy and complicated procedures for preparation. The older the pickle the better it is.

Coriander or Mint Chutney (Dhaniya ya Pudina ki Chutey)

1 cup chopped coriander or mint
2 lemons juice extracted
1 teaspoon salt
3-4 hot green chillies
1 small onion
$\frac{1}{2}''$ piece of ginger peeled and chopped fine
2 cloves garlic

Pick and wash the coriander or mint, discarding the hard
stems. Grind all the ingredients together finely and pour out into
a bowl to serve as a dip or as an accompaniment to a meal
or fried foods. In this recipe you could substitute tamarind pulp
for lemon juice. If doing so, soak a piece of tamarind about
$2'' \times 2'' \times 2''$ in water for a couple of hours. The water should be
just enough to cover it. Separate seeds and squeeze out the pulp.
Strain through a sieve. Add instead of lemon juice.

Cashew Chutney (Kaju Ki Chutney)

1 cup cashews
1″ piece ginger
2 hot green chillies
1 teaspoon salt
Juice of 1 lemon
A few leaves of mint or coriander

Blend together all the ingredients to a smooth paste. Serve
as a dip for fried baras, pakoras, fish, salad or as an accompaniment to a meal.

Raisin Chutney

1 cup raisins
Juice of 2 lemons
1 teaspoon salt
1″ piece of ginger
2 green chillies

Grind together all the ingredients to a smooth paste. Serve
as a dip or as an accompaniment to a meat dish. This is a kind
of sweet and sour chutney.

Ginger and Garlic Chutney (Adrak aur Lasan Chutney)

½ cup chopped ginger
4-6 cloves garlic
2 green chillies
1 tablespoon sugar
1 teaspoon salt
Juice of 2 lemons

Grind together all the ingredients and serve as an accompaniment to a meal or as a dip with very mild fried foods because it

is a hot chutney and a little amount goes a long way.

Pomegranate Seed Chutney (Anardana Chutney)

1 cup anardana
1 teaspoon chillie powder
½ teaspoon celery seeds
½ cup raisins
2 cloves
1″ piece of ginger
Salt to taste
Juice of a lemon

Soak anardana overnight. Grind together all the ingredients to as smooth a paste as possible. This chutney tends to be coarse as the anardana seeds will not blend to a smooth consistency. Served with plain parathas or fried foods or taken by itself it improves digestion.

Dried Plum Chutney (Alu Bukhara Chutney)

½ cup dates (pitted)
1½ cups dried plums (Alu bukhara)
1 tablespoon salt (preferably black salt)
1 teaspoon roasted cumin seeds ground
1 teaspoon garam masala
½ cup brown sugar or gur (jaggery)
2 tablespoons vinegar
3 cups water
½″ piece ginger crushed
10 almonds
10 pistachio nuts
10 cashewnuts
½ cup raisins

Soak the dried plums in 3 cups water overnight. Chop the dates finely. Blanch the almonds and shred fine. Also shred the cashews fine.

Boil the soaked plums in the same water until the seeds are easily removed. Cool, mash and pass the mixture through a sieve, add sugar or gur, shredded nuts, raisins, salt, ginger, vinegar and garam masala and cook over medium heat until consistency thickens. Add ground cumin powder, mix well and store in a sterilised bottle. Once cooled leave in the fridge. It should last about a week.

Tamarind Chutney (Imli Chutney)

1 cup tamarind
1 tablespoon salt (black salt preferably)
1 teaspoon roasted cumin seeds ground
1½ tablespoons brown sugar or gur
1 teaspoon hot chillie powder

Soak the tamarind overnight in as much water as will just cover it. Boil and pass the mixture through a sieve or cheesecloth to remove strings and seeds. Add sugar, salt, chillie powder and cumin and boil down to a thick pulp. Keeps for about a week if stored in the fridge.

Coconut Chutney (Narial Ki Chutney)

½ coconut fresh, chopped fine
2-4 green chillies, chopped fine
½" piece of ginger, chopped fine
1 teaspoon salt
Juice of 1 lemon

Grind together all the ingredients to a creamy white, rough textured mixture. Serve with pakoras or as a dip or as an accompaniment to a meal.

Mango Chutney (Aam Ki Chutney)

2 lb mangoes
2 cups vinegar
1 cup raisins
2 teaspoons mustard seeds
4 cups sugar
4-6 green chillies chopped fine
2" piece ginger grated
4-6 garlic cloves crushed
1 teaspoon salt+10 peppercorns
1 teaspoon cumin seeds + 1 teaspoon coriander seeds, crushed peppercorns and coriander seeds.

Mix 1 cup vinegar, sugar, chilles, ginger, garlic, mustard

seeds, salt and cumin seeds and cook for 1 minute. Keep aside. Peel and chop the mangoes into medium-sized chunks. Mix 1 cup vinegar and boil for 5 minutes. Add spiced vinegar and cook on medium heat for about 45 minutes. As it starts to thicken take care that it does not stick to the bottom of the pot Add raisins and stir briskly until quite thick but not mushy. Pour into sterilized jars and store. Serve with breads when needed. Once opened, the jam should be refrigerated.

The above method can be used for making chutney with other fruits also, like plums, apples, pears, peaches or apricots or mixed fruit, substituting the fruit for mango in the recipe.

Tomato Chutney (Tamatar Ki Chutney)

2 lb ripe tomatoes
2 large onions, chopped + 4 cloves garlic
2 tablespoons salt + 1 pinch of sodium benzoate
2 tablespoons sugar, brown preferred
1 teaspoon dried ginger
2 tablespoons kishmish
1 teaspoon red chillie powder
1 teaspoon cumin seeds crushed
2 tablespoons white vinegar
½ teaspoon ground coriander seeds
1 teaspoon crushed dill seeds

Wash and cut the tomatoes; add onion, garlic, ginger, kishmish, red chillies, cumin seeds and coriander and simmer on slow fire for 15-20 minutes. Add sugar, vinegar, salt and dill seeds and cook until a thick, creamy consistency is obtained Remove from the fire and add one pinch of sodium benzoate and pour into sterilized jars. Use this sauce for making pizzas, or as a relish. Keeps well under refrigeration after the jar is opened.

Green Tomato Chutney

6 large green tomatoes
1 tablespoon mustard or corn oil
½ teaspoon turmeric
6 hot green chillies chopped fine
1″ piece of ginger grated
1 teaspoon cumin seeds

1 teaspoon garam masala
1 teaspoon salt
½ cup water
2 tablespoons lemon sugar
½ cup vinegar
1 pinch asafoetida powder

Clean, wash and cut the tomatoes into chunks. Heat the oil and add asafoetida and cumin seeds until they splutter. Add ginger, green chillies, turmeric, garam masala, water, salt and tomatoes and simmer until tender. Add vinegar and lemon sugar and cook until thick, coarse consistency is obtained. Remove from the fire, cool and pour into sterilized jars. Keeps well for about 1 year. Serve as a relish with fried foods or as an accompaniment to meals.

Gooseberry Pickle (Amla ka Achar)

10-12 gooseberries
½ teaspoon chillie powder
½ teaspoon mustard powder
½ teaspoon turmeric
Salt to taste
1 pinch hing (asafoetida)
1 tablespoon mustard oil

Wash and prick the gooseberries or wash, slice and seed gooseberries. Heat the oil, add mustard, chillies, turmeric, asafoetida and gooseberries with salt. Saute for a few minutes. Remove from the fire, cool and store in an airtight jar. It will last for about 2 weeks.

Green Chillie Pickle

1 lb green chillies
1 teaspoon mustard seeds
½ teaspoon fenugreek seeds crushed
½ teaspoon turmeric (optional)
1 teaspoon salt
Juice of 2 limes
2 tablespoons mustard oil

Wash and cut the chillies into small pieces. Keep aside. Heat the oil. Add fenugreek and mustard seeds and allow to pop. Next add turmeric, chillies and salt and saute for 10 minutes. Remove from the fire and when cool add juice of 2 limes. Mix well and serve as an accompaniment to a meal. It will keep for a week.

Lime Pickle (Nimboo Achar)

2 lb lime
1 cup sugar
2 tablespoons chillie powder
2 tablespoons salt
½ teaspoon black salt
½ teaspoon asafoetida
1 teaspoon ajwain crushed coarsely

Cut each lime into 4 or 8 pieces, keeping 2 or 3 aside to squeeze out the juice. Steam the limes till semi-soft and allow to cool. Mix all the ingredients and the juice and put into a jar. Leave in the sun for a few days. The changed appearance will show that the pickle is ready for use.

Lemon Pickle

8 lemons
2 tablespoons salt
1 cup mustard oil
1 tablespoon chillie power
1 teaspoon ajwain (celery seeds)
10-12 peppercorns

Wash, dry and cut the lemons into 8 pieces each. Mix all the spices with lemon pieces and pack into a sterilized jar. Heat the oil and when smoke appears remove from the fire and pour over the lemons in the jar. Mix thoroughly and cap when cool. Place in a sunny place for about 15-20 days before using as an accompaniment to a meal. Into the same recipe you could add some green chillies also.

Lemon, Green Chillies and Ginger Pickle

6 lemons cut into 8 pieces each
Juice of 2 lemons
1 cup coarsely cut green chillies
1 cup thin sliced ginger

2 tablespoons salt
1 teaspoon celery seeds crushed
1 teaspoon black pepper or 10 peppercorns
½ teaspoon asafoetida or black salt (ground)

Mix all the ingredients thoroughly and pack tightly into a
jar. Pour the juice of 2 lemons and place the lid securely. Keep
in a sunny window for about 15-20 days before using as an
accompaniment to a meal. Shake the jar vigorously every second
day to infuse all the ingredients. It is very important to keep this
pickle in the sun. Bring the jar inside and keep in a warm place
at night. Any of the above lime or lemon pickles is a good
remedy for stomach pains and digestive disorders.

Whole Lime Pickles (Sabut Nimboo ka Achar)

20 limes
Juice of 5 limes
½ cup salt
1 teaspoon black salt
1 teaspoon celery (ajwain) crushed
6 cloves

Wash, dry and prick limes several times with a fork. Put the
limes, salt, black salt and celery into a jar and pour over the
juice. Cover tightly and leave the jar in direct sunlight for as
long as the ingredients take to get infused and the lemons are
tender and brown in colour.

This is a medicinal pickle used at times to stimulate appetite
and after long illness and nausea.

Carrot Pickle

1 lb carrots
1 tablespoon chillie powder
1 teaspoon cumin seed powder
1 tablespoon mustard (black) powder
1 tablespoon turmeric
2 tablespoons salt
1 cup mustard oil

Scrape the carrots. Wash and cut or slice into ½″ thick pieces.
Heat the oil and remove from the fire. Add mustard, turmeric and

cumin to the hot oil. Then add carrots, chillie powder and salt. Cool and pack in jars and leave in a warm, sunny place for 10 days before using as an accompaniment to a meal.

Cauliflower and Turnip Pickle (Gobi aur Shalgam Achar)

1 lb turnips
2 lb cauliflower
1 cup brown sugar or jaggery (gur)
2 tablespoons mustard seeds (black) coarsely powdered
2 tablespoons salt + 1 teaspoon black salt
2″ piece ginger grated
6-8 garlic cloves crushed
½ cup vinegar
½ cup mustard oil
1 tablespoon garam masala
4 dried whole chillies

Wash, dry, peel and cut turnips into ¼″ thick slices. Wash, pat dry and cut the cauliflower into chunks. Immerse in boiling water for 5 minutes and drain Keep in a colander for for 2 hours or so until completely dry. Heat the oil and fry garlic and ginger until golden brown. Add whole chillies and remove from the fire and keep aside. Heat the jaggery in vinegar until well dissolved. Add to it mustard, garam masala, salt and black salt. Pour over the oil with garlic and ginger. Add the turnips and cauliflower, mix well and put into a jar. Keep in the sun for 8-10 days. This pickle keeps well for a year.

Navrattan Achar (Mixed Mango, Gooseberry, Onion Pickle)

2 lb mangoes cut into slices or chunks
½ lb small white onions
½ lb karondas (sour gooseberry)
2 cups mustard oil
2 tablespoons turmeric
1 tablespoon chillie powder
½ lb ginger cut into thin, long strips
10 peppercorns crushed
1 teaspoon fenugreek seeds ground

2 large black cardamoms crushed
1 teaspoon nigella (kalonji) crushed coarsely
2 tablespoons fennel (saunf) crushed coarsely
½ teaspoon asafoetida powder
2-4 whole dried red chillies
8-10 green chillies cut into 2 pieces each

Wash, peel and cut the mangoes. Wash, dry and wipe the karondas. Heat the oil to smoking point. Add kalonji, fennel and fenugreek seeds and asafoetida. Add the mango slices, ginger strips, whole karondas, button onions, green chillies, red chillies crushed peppercorns and salt. Stir with a wooden spoon for a couple of minutes and remove from the fire. Put into sterilized jars and keep in a warm, sunny place for about 1 month before using as an accompaniment to a meal.

Mango Pickle (Aam ka Achar)

5 lb raw mangoes
2 tablespoons crushed hot red chillies
1 tablespoon fenugreek seeds ground coarsely
2 tablespoons turmeric
4 tablespoons salt
1 tablespoon black salt
2 tablespoons fennel (saunf) crushed
1 teaspoon nigella seeds (kalonji)
2 tablespoons coriander seeds crushed coarsely
4 cups mustard oil

Heat the oil until a blue haze appears. Remove from the heat and keep aside. Wash, dry and cut the mangoes into slices, strips or chunks. Mix in all the spices and put into a jar. Pour the oil over to cover the mangoes and keep in the sun for a few days. Shake every 2 days to infuse the ingredients into the mango slices well. Takes about 2 months to be ready. The pickle is ready when mango pieces are soft and the crushed spices are swollen and upon opening the jar a highly spicy aroma arises which is very peculiar to the mango pickle. Serve as an accompaniment to any meal or with plain paratha or phulka for lunch or breakfast along with lassi.

FRUIT PRESERVES (Murabba)

Murabbas, fruit jams and jellies are a favourite of all age groups. Jams and jellies were introduced in India by the British and are now very popular throughout the country. Mango, carrot, amla (gooseberry) and apple are ideal for murabbas and are very popular in Punjab. The fruit must be firm, fresh, ripe and of the best quality, if good results are to be obtained. The preparations should be made when the particular fruit or vegetable is cheap and available in abundance.

Mango Preserve (Aam Ka Murabba)

2 lb raw mangoes
2 lb sugar
1 teaspoon tartaric acid
4-5 cups water
1 teaspoon alum powder
1 teaspoon essence of kewra or rose-water
4 green cardamoms crushed

Wash, pare and slice the mangoes into large pieces Prick the pieces with a fork Soak in water, to which alum has been added. The water should be enough to cover the pieces of mango. Keep aside overnight or a few hours. Wash in cold water a couple of times and pat dry; leave aside while the syrup is being prepared.

Mix the sugar and tartaric acid in 5 cups of water and boil until it reaches one thread consistency. Add the mango slices and simmer till the syrup thickens and the slices become soft. Remove from the fire and leave covered overnight. If the syrup turns thin, boil again the next day. Sprinkle with cardamom powder and kewra essence or rose-water. Pour into jars and secure the lids. Serve with plain parathas for breakfast or as a snack.

Mango Marmalade

4 cups mango shreds (raw mangoes)
6 cups sugar
Juice of 2 lemons
1 cup mango juice
1 cup water

Wash, peel, remove stones and grate the mangoes into long

shreds. Add ½ cup water and simmer until soft. Cook the sugar and water to a one thread consistency. Add the cooked shreds and juice, lemon juice and cook, briskly stirring all the time until it reaches the jelly test stage (one spoon of mixture poured on a cold plate jells quickly). Remove from the fire and pour into sterilized jars.

Guava Jelly (Amrood Jelly)

1½ lb guavas
1½ lb sugar
Juice of 4 lemons
3 cups water

Wash the guavas, slice and mix with water and cook on medium heat until the fruit is soft and liquid thick. Strain through a cheesecloth to remove the seeds. To the strained juice add sugar and simmer until thick. Add the lemon juice and continue cooking until it reaches the jelly stage. Pour into sterilized jars and allow to cool before securing the lids on the jars.

Spiced Guava Preserve

1 lb guavas
1 lb sugar
Juice of 2 lemons
2 cups water
1 tablespoon fennel (saunf) crushed coarsely
1 tablespoon salt
8-10 peppercorns

Wash, slice and cook the fruit with water, fennel seeds, peppercorns and salt. When it is thick and the fruit is soft, add lemon juice and sugar and continue to cook until a thick and rough texture is obtained. Remove from the fire, cool and pour into jars. It is very delicious eaten with plain parathas or puri.

Carrot Preserve (Gajjar Ka Murabba)

1 lb carrots (baby carrots preferred)
1 lb sugar
1 cup water
½ teaspoon citric acid

Scrape and wash the carrots and slit into halves. Prick all over with fork and soak in some cold water for a couple of hours Drain out the water leaving only 1 cup. Add sugar and citric acid. Simmer on low fire until carrots become soft and the syrup is of one thread consistency. Remove from the fire and allow to cool before pouring into jars to store away. Serve as an accompaniment to a meal, as a dessert or just as a snack.

Pineapple Jam (Ananas ka Jam)

2 lb pineapple
1 lb sugar
½ cup of water
Juice of 2 limes

Peel the pineapple being careful to remove the eyes with a sharp knife. Scrape or cut into 1″ cubes. Add ½ cup water, sugar and lime juice and allow to cook on medium heat until it thickens. Before the sugar reaches one thread consistency, remove from the fire, cool and pour into jars. Secure the lids tightly.

Apple Murabba

2 lb Granny Smith or cooking apples
2 lb sugar
2¼ cups water
Juice of 2 lemons
2 cardamoms
1″ piece cinnamon stick
2-4 cloves

Wash, peel and core the apples. Mix together water, sugar and spices and boil until the sugar is dissolved. Add the apples and simmer until the syrup is thick and of one thread consistency. Add the lemon juice and cook for another 2-3 minutes. Remove from the fire, cool a little and seal into jars a few at a time, allowing one clove and one cardamom to go into each jar.

Peaches or Crab Apples in Syrup

3 cups sugar
1½ cups vinegar
1½ cups water

1″ stick cinnamon
2 lb peaches or crab apples
1 tablespoon whole allspice or peppercorn

Mix sugar, vinegar, water and spices and boil the mixture for half an hour. Immerse the whole fruit (cleaned and washed) in water and cook until just tender. Remove the fruit with a spoon and put into warm jars. Pour the syrup into them and fill the jar completely. Securely seal the lid.

Stuffed, Hot Red Pepper Pickle (Bharvi Mirch Achar)

1 kg hot red peppers
250 gm amchur (dried mango powder)
250 gm sarsoo (black mustard)
100 gm garam masala
100 gm celery seeds (ajwain)
50 gm fenugreek (methi)
250 gm salt
1 kg mustard oil

Pick, clean and grind all the spices. Wash and dry the peppers. Cut off stems and clean the insides allowing the seeds to be mixed in with the spices. Mix the spices in 2 tablespoons oil and stuff into the peppers. Keep in the sun for a couple of days to dry. Pack into sterilized jars and pour the oil to cover completely. Secure the lid tightly and place in a sunny location. Leave 6-8 weeks for spices to swell and infuse well. Shake every few days.

Whole Lime Pickle (Sabat Nimboo Achar)

1 kg limes (ripe, firm and yellow)
1 kg salt (coarse)

Soak the limes in water for 6-7 days, changing the water every-day. Wipe dry and have a wide mouthed jar ready. Place some salt to cover the bottom of the jar. Arrange a layer of limes and sprinkle with salt. Repeat the process till the jar is full and top-most layer is of salt. Secure the lid tightly and leave in a sunny place. Do not shake this particular achar; allow it to mature for several months before using as an accompaniment to a meal. It is ready when the outer shell is soft.

Spiced Whole Lime Pickle (Masallewala Nimboo da Achar)

1 kg yellow, firm limes
½ kg salt
250 gm sugar
100 gm celery seeds (ajwain)
2 cups vinegar
1 cup water
½ cup corn oil

Clean and wash the limes. Prick several limes and pack into a sterilized jar. Boil together vinegar, corn oil, water and spices for a few minutes. Pour on to the packed limes and allow to cool. Secure the lid tightly and keep in a sunny place for a couple of months. Shake occasionally to infuse the ingredients.

Pickled Cucumber and Dills (Kheera da Achar)

3 cups water
3 cups vinegar
1 cup sugar
½ cup salt
2 tablespoons pickling spices
1 kg cucumber
A few sprigs of dill
2 tablespoon alum

Select tender cucumbers. If you like to pickle them whole, select small-sized ones. Wash, dry and slice the cucumbers. Soak the cucumbers overnight in alum water, which should be just enough to cover them. The next day wash with lots of cold water and allow to drain. Pack lightly into sterilized jars. Prepare the base by boiling water, vinegar, sugar, salt and spices for 10 minutes. Place a sprig of dill into each jar and pour the vinegar base to cover cucumbers properly. Seal lightly and sterilize either in the oven or in boiling water. Remove and secure the lids tightly. Place in a dark place for a couple of weeks before using it with sandwiches or any meal.

Mixed Garden Pickle (Bagicha Ralya Milya Achar)

1 cup sliced cucumbers
1 cup sliced onions

1 cup chopped peppers
1 cup chopped green tomatoes
1 cup chopped carrots
1 cup chopped green beans
1 cup chopped celery
1 cup chopped cabbage
2 cups sugar
½ cup salt
1 tablespoon celery seeds
1 tablespoon garam masala

Cook carrots and beans in boiling water for 5 minutes, drain well and keep aside. Soak cucumbers, onion, peppers tomatoes, cabbage and celery in salt water overnight. Wash with cold water and drain well. Mix with carrots and beans. Boil vinegar, sugar, garam masala and celery seeds. Add all the vegetables and boil for 15 minutes or until the liquid evaporates. Pack into sterilised jars and secure lids tightly. Serve as an accompaniment to grilled cheese sandwiches, hot dogs, hamburgers or any other fried food. Before securing lids, pour into it a couple of tablespoons of corn oil or vegetable oil which helps to preserve it for a longer period.

You could try making this as a cucumber relish or pickle with vegetables except pepper and celery and using 6 cups of corn taken off the tender cobs. My very favourite combination of vegetables is pepper and celery greens served along with either an Indian meal or western meal; it will do justice as long as you like corn.

Cucumber Relish (Kheera Achar)

4 cups minced cucumbers
2 cups celery stalks, trimmed and minced fine
2 cups sugar
4 cups vinegar
4 tablespoons dry mustard
1 tablespoon turmeric
½ cup pickling spices
½ cup all-purpose flour
½ cup salt

Mix together onions, cucumbers and celery; sprinkle with salt and leave overnight. Drain all the water and keep aside. Combine vinegar, flour, pickling spices, turmeric, mustard and boil well. Add the vegetables and cook on low fire until the vegetables are tender and soft and mixture thickenes. Ladle into sterilized jars and secure tightly. You could omit flour if you intend to store it for a longer period.

Index